A guide to lei

KENT SURREY

SUSSEX

SERIES EDITOR CATHERINE BAKER

·K·U·P·E·R·A·R·D·

Going Places

Going Places – the most comprehensive coverage in one volume of the leisure and sporting activities to be enjoyed in the cities, towns and villages of these adjoining counties. An invaluable source of information and ideas for visitors and residents alike, this guide offers all age groups the opportunity to pursue a favourite pastime or discover a new one regardless of the weather or season.

The activities section gives you detailed information on over sixty leisure activities, the names and addresses of their governing bodies and a list of all the places where you can enjoy them, arranged alphabetically under county headings. To find out more details look up the places in the second section of the guide.

The second section is a comprehensive gazetteer of one hundred places in the region. You will find a description, some local information and a detailed list of all the leisure activities with the telephone number, address or access information and any other interesting details. It couldn't be easier.

First published in the UK by:
Kuperard (London) Ltd,
30 Cliff Road,
London NW1 9AG

First published 1991
© Research and text
J & J Entertainment Ltd.
© Design and production
The Pen & Ink Book Company Ltd.

ISBN 1-870668-56-1
Design and production

**PEN
INK**

Printed and bound
in Great Britain

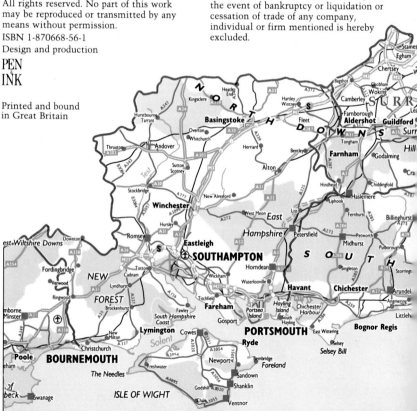

Acknowledgements

We are very grateful for the help we have received from the county, district and local councils, the tourist information centres and the individual establishments we have included in this guide. Every effort has been made to obtain accurate details at the time of going to press, however it is advisable that you telephone your destination before embarking on a long journey. Corrections, alterations or additional entries should be sent to The Editor, c/o The Publisher, for inclusion in a new edition.

We would like to thank the following for supplying the photographs included in this guide:

Abbey Stadium Sports Centre; Chris Ridgers; County Visuals, Kent County Council; Gloucestershire County Planning Department; Hereford & Worcester County Council, Department of Engineering and Planning;

Ian Meredith; Kym Bannister; Mid Suffolk Leisure Centre; Mike Shackleton; Solar Wings Limited; South East England Tourist Board; Sportsphoto Agency; Suffolk Coastal District Council; Tim Cox

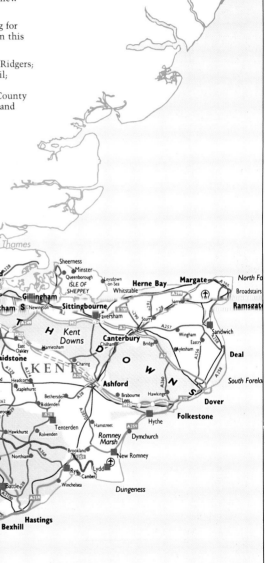

Contents

Activities

However you like to spend your time, whether ballooning or birdwatching, microlight flying or messing about in boats, playing a round of golf or soaking up the history and tradition found in historic houses, churches and castles, then Kent, Surrey and Sussex have much to offer. Everything is listed in this section. Look up the leisure or sporting activity you are interested in, they are arranged alphabetically, and you will find a list of all the locations where you can pursue your interest, these are again listed alphabetically. To find out more details about these venues look up the town or village in the second section and under the relevant activity heading you will find the telephone number, address or access information and more details. It couldn't be easier and browsing through these pages you might even discover a new sport or activity to try, as well as a new appreciation and enjoyment of the leisure facilities offered in these counties.

Shooting

Shooting, whether rifle, game or clay pigeon shooting, is a popular sport for many. Gun licences are required by anyone owning or using a rifle or shotgun, they are obtained from the police headquarters or the Chief Constable of your area of residence. Game licences are required for certain quarry; pheasant, deer, grouse and partridge for instance, but not for rabbits provided permission has previously been obtained from the landowner or owner of the shooting rights. Game licences can be obtained from local post offices before shooting. Rifle clubs and sporting agencies will usually organise gun and game licences when necessary.

More detailed information about shooting and clay pigeon shooting can be obtained from the associations listed below.

British Association for Shooting and Conservation
National Headquarters
Marford Mill
Clwyd
☎ 0244 570881

Clay Pigeon Shooting Association
107 Epping New Road
Buckhurst Hill
Essex
☎ 081 505 6221

SURREY

Caterham: Copthorne Gun Club

KENT

Lullingstone: Brands Hatch Circuit and Activity Centre

SUSSEX

East Grinstead: Horne Clay Pigeon Club

Aerial Sports

Ballooning

The romantic appeal of hot air ballooning captivates many – if the idea of drifting through bright, clear skies appeals then this might be the pursuit for you. To gain your private pilot's licence tuition from a qualified pilot is necessary. A minimum of twelve hours flying experience and a test flight with a qualified examiner are the prerequisites necessary for you to make a solo flight. Additional examinations in navigation, meteorology, and air law will safely extend your ballooning skills.

The British Ballooning and Airship Club is the governing body of the sport and they will provide information on ballooning meets and local clubs.

The British Ballooning and Airship Club
Barbara Green, Information Officer
P.O. Box 1006
Birmingham
☎ 021 643 3224

SURREY

Esher: Lindsay Muir
Farnham: Airship Shop Ltd

Flying

To take to the skies has been man's aspiration for centuries and the appeal of flying never seems to diminish. To obtain a private pilot's licence requires a minimum of 40 hours flight training at a local flying club, five multiple-choice examinations in meteorology, aviation law, technical aspects, radio telephony and navigation and two flight tests with an examiner to observe both general handling and navigational skills. For anyone interested in taking up flying the Student Pilots Association, whose address is listed below, will supply both information and a list of flying schools on request.

For those who either own a plane or who might be interested in building a plane then the Popular Flying Association will be a valuable source of information, their address is below.

Student Pilots Association
30 Tisbury Road
Hove
East Sussex
☎ 0273 204080

Popular Flying Association
Terminal Building
Shoreham Airport
Shoreham-by-Sea
☎ 0273 461616

KENT

Biggin Hill: Air Touring Club; Biggin Hill School of Flying; Kingair School of Flying; Surrey and Kent Flying Club
Chatham: Rochester Aviation Flying Club

Lydd: London Flight Centre; South East College of Air Training
Maidstone: London Flight Centre

SURREY

Camberley: Blackbushe School of Flying; Three Counties Aero Club
Chertsey: Fairoaks Flying Club
Reigate: Redhill Flying Club

SUSSEX

Chichester: Goodwood Aerodrome
Shoreham-by-Sea: Mercury Flying Club; Southern Aero Club; Southern Air

Gliding

Gliding is a graceful and exciting way to explore the skies. Learning to control a glider is easily and quickly mastered whilst learning to soar is the art every glider pilot seeks. A skilful pilot can cover over two hundred miles or climb to tens of thousands of feet.

Trial flights are available to give you a taste of the air and no age restrictions exist other than pilots under sixteen not being able to fly solo. Dual-control training gliders are used for training and an average of 50 take-offs and landings accompanied by a qualified instructor will take you to solo flying standard. To fly cross-country you must acquire your Bronze badge which will test not only your flying ability but also your knowledge of air law, meteorology and the theory of flight.

The governing body of gliding is the British Gliding Association. They will provide you with information about gliding and details of gliding clubs.

The British Gliding Association
Kimberley House
Vaughan Way
Leicester
☎ 0533 531051

Caterham: Surrey Hills Gliding Club

KENT

Ashford: Kent Gliding Club
Dover: Channel Gliding Club

SUSSEX

Lewes: East Sussex Gliding Club

Hang Gliding

Hang gliding has an element of adventure and excitement. All the senses are used to master three planes of movement simultaneously when you 'take to the skies'. Hang gliding attracts people of all ages and backgrounds – the minimum age to fly solo is 16, there is no maximum age. Basic training at a school registered with the British Hang Gliding Association (BHGA) is the first step to solo flying. A minimum of a week's course is required to obtain the Pilot One licence needed to fly your own hang glider. The BHGA set out and maintain high standards of instruction, equipment and service at the 21 schools registered with them.

The governing body of hang gliding is the British Hang Gliding Association listed below. Information about hang gliding and a list of registered schools is available from them on request.

**British Hang Gliding Association
(BHGA)**
Cranfield Airfield
Cranfield
Bedfordshire
☎ 0234 751688

SUSSEX

Biggin Hill: Skyriders
Brighton: Sussex College of Hang
 Gliding
Hove: Free Flight

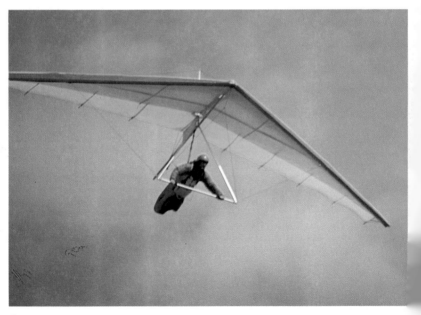

Microlight Flying

Microlights are small aircraft that are great fun to fly. They are single or two seater hi-tech planes that have been flown as far afield as Africa and Australia and at speeds of over 100 mph. They are definitely not toy aeroplanes yet they need none of the facilities of a conventional aeroplane – your garage can be your hangar and any fair-sized field your aerodrome. If you are interested try an 'air experience' flight from one of the listed schools. Learning to fly then involves a training course to acquire your flying licence, this usually takes between one and six months. You need to be 17 and reasonably fit to fly your own microlight. Patience and perseverance will enable you to learn the art of flying so you can escape into the air and enjoy this safe and exhilarating form of flight.

The British Microlight Association is the governing body of the sport and can be contacted for more information at the address below.

British Microlight Aircraft Association
Bullring
Deddington
Oxford
☎ 0869 38888

Margate: Kent Microlight and Aircraft Club
Rochester: Medway Microlight Club

KENT

Canterbury: Kent Microlight and Aircraft Club; South East Microlight Aircraft Centre

SURREY

Leatherhead: The Surrey Microlight Club

9

Parachuting

Parachuting is exciting, exhilarating and dynamic; it offers you the joy and freedom of the sky. You can experience the thrill of your first jump by static line parachuting where your parachute opens automatically as soon as you leave the aircraft, by accelerated free-fall (AFF) where your first descent is from 12,000 feet with two highly qualified instructors, or by tandem parachuting where you jump using a dual harness system with an instructor who controls your free-fall and landing – a quick and easy introduction to free-fall. You can progress from beginner to complete parachutist by one of two systems depending on how you made your first jump, and then go on to take up sport parachuting, a highly skilled sport offering many personal and competitive challenges.

The British Parachute Association is the governing body of the sport and will supply you with information both about the sport and courses offered by its affiliated clubs.

The British Parachute Association
Mr D Oddy (National Administrator)
5 Wharf Way
Glen Parva
Leicester
☎ 0533 785271

KENT

Ashford: Headcorn Parachute Centre; Slipstream Adventures

SUSSEX

Chichester: Flying Tigers Skydiving Centre

Paragliding

Paragliding or parascending is parachuting without an aircraft. Parascenders are tow-launched over land and water or foot-launched from a hillside to experience the exhilaration of flying under a canopy, square or round. You can join an introductory course at one of the British Association of Parascending Clubs where you will be given thorough ground training as well as learning how to fly yourself – usually in a day. Further courses are tailor-made to local conditions and your choice – you can learn to make flights last for hours, try aerobatics or take part in competitions, meets or fun events. Whatever you do there will be a qualified BAPC expert to supervise and help you decide within strict safety guidelines. Parascending is an exciting and inexpensive sport that will place the world at your feet.

The British Association of Parascending Clubs, the governing body of the sport, will provide details of their clubs and a full information pack on request.

British Association of Parascending Clubs Ltd
18 Talbot Lane
Leicester
☎ 0533 530318

KENT

Lullingstone: Brands Hatch Circuit and Activity Centre
Ramsgate: Seawide Leisure

Badminton

Badminton is another of the racket sports that remains popular. There are plenty of opportunities to play in the many leisure and sports centres throughout the region. For information about badminton and details of local clubs contact the Badminton Association of England, whose address is below.

Badminton Association of England
National Badminton Centre
Bradwell Road
Loughton Lodge
Milton Keynes
☎ 0908 568822

SURREY

Leatherhead: Leatherhead Leisure Centre

KENT

Bromley: National Sports Centre
Gillingham: Medway Badminton Association
Margate: Hartsdown Park Sports and Leisure Centre; Lonsdale Court Sports Centre

SUSSEX

Crawley: Bewbush Leisure Centre
Hastings: Summerfields Sports Centre
Horsham: Park Recreation Centre
Littlehampton: The Badminton & Squash Club

Leisure Centres

Excellent opportunities exist throughout the region to pursue a range of indoor sports options including the increasingly popular racket sports of squash and badminton as well as ice skating, roller skating and tenpin bowling. For the fit, not so fit and those who wish to relax there are the more varied facilities offered by the sports and leisure centres listed, these include saunas, solariums, fitness centres, swimming pools, splash pools, badminton courts and bodybuilding gyms. The range of facilities offered by different leisure centres is so diverse that it would be advisable to contact individual centres to discover what they offer.

KENT

Bromley: Beckenham Leisure Centre; Bromley Sports Hall; National Sports Centre; Walnut Sports Centre
Dover: Dover Sports Centre
Folkestone: Folkestone Sports Centre
Gillingham: Black Lion Leisure Centre; Centre Sports Priestfield; The Strand Leisure Park
Gravesend: Cascades Leisure Centre
Herne Bay: Pier Pavilion
Maidstone: Maidstone Leisure Centre; Westborough Sports Centre; YMCA Sports Centre
Margate: Hartsdown Park Sports and Leisure Centre

Northfleet: Cygnet Leisure Centre
Rochester: Maidstone Road Sports
Centre; Strood Sports Centre
Royal Tunbridge Wells: Sports and 'Y'
Centre
Sevenoaks: Wildernesse Sports Centre
Sheerness: Sheppey Leisure Centre
Sittingbourne: The Swallows
Whitstable: Sports Centre

Banstead: Banstead Sports Centre
Camberley: Arena Leisure Centre
Caterham: De Stafford School; Oxted
County School Sports Hall
Egham: Spelthorne Leisure Centre
Epsom: Rainbow Centre
Farnham: Farnham Sports Centre
Godalming: Godalming Leisure Centre
Guildford: Guildford Sports Centre;
University of Surrey Sports Hall
Leatherhead: Leatherhead Leisure
Centre
Reigate: Donyngs Recreation Centre
Walton-on-Thames: Elmbridge Leisure
Centre
Woking: Horsell Recreation Centre;
The Winston Churchill Recreation
Centre; Woking Leisure Centre

Bexhill-on-Sea: Bexhill Leisure Centre
Bognor Regis: Arun Leisure Centre
Brighton: Stanley Deason Leisure
Centre; Withdean Sports Complex
Chichester: Southern Leisure Centre;
Westgate
Crawley: Crawley Leisure Centre
Crowborough: Goldsmiths Leisure
Centre
Eastbourne: Cavendish Sports Centre;
Hampden Park Sports Centre;
Sundowners Leisure Centre
East Grinstead: Kings Centre
Hastings: Summerfields Sports Centre
Haywards Heath: Dolphin Leisure
Centre
Horsham: Broadbridge Heath Leisure
Centre; Forest Recreation Centre;
Park Recreation Centre
Hove: King Alfred Leisure Centre
Littlehampton: Swimming & Sports
Centre
Newhaven: Meridian Leisure Centre;
Tideway Leisure Centre
Seaford: Downs Leisure Centre
Worthing: Worthing Leisure Centre;
Davison Leisure Centre

ICE SKATING

Bromley: Beckenham Leisure Centre
Gillingham: Gillingham Ice Bowl
Margate: Hartsdown Park Sports and
Leisure Centre
Northfleet: Sprints

TEN PIN BOWLING

Margate: Top Ten Bowling
Whitstable: Whitstable Bowl

ICE SKATING

Brighton: Sussex Ice Rink
Hastings: White Rock Ice Rink

TEN PIN BOWLING

Bexhill-on-Sea: GX Superbowl
Crawley: Crawley Bowl
Hove: King Alfred Leisure Centre
Worthing: Worthing Bowl

Squash

Squash is one of the racket sports that has flourished over the last twenty years, a popular sport for the busy executive or for the sports enthusiast who enjoys the challenge it provides and the fitness it requires. Squash courts are a prominent feature of most leisure and sports centres and many hotels offer squash facilities so it is unlikely that you will ever be far away from somewhere to play.

KENT

Bromley: Leisure Centres
Herne Bay: Pier Pavilion
Maidstone: Westborough Sports Centre
Margate: Dreamland Squash Club
Ramsgate: Dumpton Stadium
Whitstable: West Beach

Haslemere: Haslemere Swimming Pool and Squash Courts
Leatherhead: Leatherhead Leisure Centre
Reigate: Donyngs Recreation Centre
Walton-on-Thames: Elmbridge Leisure Centre
Woking: Woking Squash Rackets Club

SURREY

Dorking: Dorking Lawn Tennis and Squash Club; Dorking Town Squash Club; Friends Provident Squash Club
Esher: Sandown Park Squash Club
Farnham: Bourne Club; Farnham Sports Centre
Godalming: Guildford and Godalming Rugby Club
Guildford: University of Surrey Sports Hall

SUSSEX

Crawley: Bewbush Leisure Centre; Crawley Leisure Centre
Crowborough: Crowborough Tennis and Squash Club; Goldsmiths Leisure Centre
Eastbourne: Hampden Park Sports Centre; Sundowners Leisure Centre
East Grinstead: Kings Centre
Hastings: Summerfields Sports Centre
Haywards Heath: Dolphin Leisure Centre

Adventure Centres

Choose from a wide range of sports and activities to build up your own programme at one of the special interest or multi-activity centres listed. The range of activities offered by multi-activity centres is diverse whilst special interest centres cater for one activity or type of activity. Accommodation and prices vary so send a brochure to compare facilities before you make your choice.

The British Activity Holiday Association monitors instruction and safety standards, they offer a consumer advisory service that can be contacted via the address given below.

Special activity break packages for families are offered by many hotels and guesthouses, details of these have not been included but can be obtained from the local Tourist Information Centres.

British Activity Holiday Association
Norton Terrace
Llandrindod Wells
Powys
Wales
☎ 0597 823902

Gillingham: Barn Owl Travel
Maidstone: Kent Institute of Art and Design
Margate: Garden of England Cycling Holidays
Rochester: Medway Cruising School
Sevenoaks: Samuel Palmer School of Fine Art

KENT

MULTI-ACTIVITY CENTRES

Ashford: Hazel Tree Farm
Bromley: The Field Study Centre
Deal: East Kent Field Centre
Folkestone: Folkestone Activity Holiday Centre
Lullingstone: Brands Hatch Circuit and Activity Centre
Rochester: Arethusa Venture Centre
Royal Tunbridge Wells: Bowles Outdoor Centre
Tonbridge: Swattenden Centre; Tonbridge School

SPECIAL INTEREST CENTRES

Ashford: Rooting St Farm Riding Centre
Canterbury: British School of Falconry; Summer Academy

SURREY

MULTI-ACTIVITY CENTRES

Woking: Freetime Leisure

SPECIAL INTEREST CENTRES

Dorking: Coomb Farmhouse Countryside Training Centre
Esher: The Haven Hotel
Farnham: Hogs Back Hotel
Godalming: Inn on the Lake
Guildford: Hurtwood Inn

SUSSEX

SPECIAL INTEREST CENTRES

Chichester: The Earnley Concourse
Crowborough: The English Language and Equestrian Centre
Pulborough: The Old Rectory Adult Education College

Birdwatching

Birdlife in Britain is varied and birdwatching is an extremely popular activity as borne out by the current membership figures of the Royal Society for the Protection of Birds (RSPB) – over half a million. The RSPB have many reserves, often exceptionally beautiful locations where visitors can enjoy the relaxing atmosphere and observe the wealth of birds and wildlife from covered hides. The RSPB will supply information about their reserves, about bird watching holidays and their work on request from the address given below.

The Royal Society for the Protection of Birds (RSPB)
The Lodge
Sandy
Bedfordshire
☎ 0767 680551

KENT

Dungeness: Boulderwall
Faversham: South Swale Nature Reserve
Gillingham: Barn Owl Travel; Riverside Country Park
Ramsgate: Pegwell Bay
Rochester: Northward Hill
Sevenoaks: Bough Beech Nature Reserve

Sheerness: Elmley Marshes Nature Reserve
Sittingbourne: Queendown Warren Nature Reserve

SURREY

Haslemere: Frensham Common

SUSSEX

Arundel: Wildfowl and Wetlands Centre
Chichester: The Earnley Concourse
East Grinstead: Spring Hill Wildfowl Park; Weir Wood Reservoir
Shoreham-by-Sea: British Trust for Ornithology

Camping & Caravanning

Camping and caravanning have long been enjoyed by families and individuals of all ages as an inviting way of getting out into the countryside. The Camping and Caravanning Club will supply details about membership and their activities on request.

The Camping and Caravanning Club
Mr C A Smith (Director General)
Greenfield House
Westwood Way
Coventry
☎ 0203 694995

KENT

Deal: Leisurescope Deal
Dover: Hawthorn Farm
Dymchurch: Dymchurch Caravan Park;
E & J Piper Caravan Park
Faversham: Painters Farm Camping and
Caravan Site
Folkestone: Black Horse Farm Caravan
and Camping Park; Little
Switzerland Caravan Park; The
Warren Camping and Caravanning
Club Site
Herne Bay: Hillborough Caravan Park;
Westbrook Farm Caravan Park
Hythe: Beach Bank Caravan Park
Lamberhurst: Cedar Gables
Minster: Horseshoe Caravan Park;
Leysdown Coastal Park Camp Site;
Seacliff Holiday Estates

New Romney: New Romney Caravan
Sites Ltd
Ramsgate: Manston Caravan and
Camping Park
Rochester: Woolmans Wood Tourist
Caravan Park
Sandwich: Sandwich Leisure Park
Whitstable: Limberlost Park

SURREY

Dorking: Camping and Caravanning
Club Site

SUSSEX

Crowborough: Crowborough Caravan
and Camping Site
Petworth: Camping and Caravanning
Club Site
Pevensey: Camping and Caravanning
Club Site
Shoreham-by-Sea: Harwoods Farm

17

Cricket

Cricket conjures up images of English village greens on lazy Sunday afternoons in summer for people throughout the world. The tradition of county cricket in England is long and distinguished and can be appreciated and enjoyed by a visit to any of the county grounds. You might even be lucky enough to see some records shattered if the summers continue to be long and dry.

KENT

Canterbury: County Cricket Club

SUSSEX

Hove: Sussex County Cricket Club

Cycling

Cycling is a wonderful way of exploring this region's rich and varied countryside. Cycles are often available for hire, several cycle shops are listed in this guide and others may be listed in leaflets available from the Tourist Information Centres who also produce maps and cycle routes for many areas. Some of the cycling holiday centres will provide a luggage porter and many offer cycling weekends to give you a taste of the 'cyclers' view of the countryside – a good introduction.

The Cyclists' Touring Club, listed below, will provide touring information, information about local cycling groups as well as technical and legal information.

The Cyclists' Touring Club
69 Meadrow
Godalming
Surrey
☎ 048341 7217

KENT

Bromley: Crystal Palace to Bromley
  Cycle Route; National Sports Centre
Folkestone: Renham's
Margate: The Bike Shed; Ken's Bike
  Shop

SURREY

Godalming: Cyclists' Touring Club

SUSSEX

Arundel: Cycling Round West Sussex
Eastbourne: South Down Cycles

18

Falconry

Birds of prey fascinate and thrill with their flight and swooping precision. The ancient art of keeping and training these proud birds to return from flight or to hunt quarry is equally fascinating and can be seen in practice at the falconry centres in this region.

KENT

Canterbury: British School of Falconry
Chilham: Chilham Castle Gardens

Fishing

Fishing in Britain is divided into coarse fishing, game fishing and sea fishing. Coarse fishing is very popular, the species usually caught are bream, carp, chub, dace, gudgeon, perch, pike, roach, rudd and tench. There are many fine opportunities for excellent coarse fishing in this region, the Rivers Thames, Arun, Medway and Stour being particularly good. The close season for coarse fishing is between March 15th and June 15th. Permission in the form of a rod licence is necessary from the water authority in charge of the water you are planning to fish, these are usually obtainable from local tackle shops and are issued by the National Rivers Authority for rivers and by the Regional Water Company for still waters such as lakes and reservoirs. After obtaining the rod licence permission must be obtained from the owner of the water, this might be an angling club in which case it is usual to pay a membership fee or it might mean buying a ticket, again local tackle shops are usually the best places to enquire about water ownership.

The south-eastern counties are not noted for their game fishing waters but there are opportunities to fish for trout at some of the region's reservoirs. The close season for trout lasts from October 1st to March 24th and for salmon between November 1st and January 31st although these could vary depending on the different water authorities.

General information, licences and leaflets are available from the National Rivers Authority, Thames and Southern regions, their addresses are given below. The National Anglers' Council will also provide information about fishing in the area.

National Rivers Authority
Thames Region
King's Meadow House
King's Meadow Road
Reading
☎ 0734 535000

National Rivers Authority
Thames Region
Guildborne House
Chatsworth Road
Worthing
West Sussex
☎ 0903 820692

National Anglers' Council
Coarse Fishing ☎ 0332 362000
Game Fishing ☎ 071 283 5838
Sea Fishing ☎ 0626 331330

KENT

COARSE FISHING
Ashford: River Stour; Chequer Tree Farm; Singleton Lake
Bromley: Keston Ponds; Crystal Palace Lake

19

Canterbury: River Stour
Chatham: Capstone Country Park
Dartford: River Darent
Edenbridge: River Medway;
  Chiddingstone Castle
Faversham: Faversham Angling Club;
  Oare Pits
Hythe: Brockhill Country Park
Maidstone: Abbey Court Lake; River
  Medway; Mote Park Lake
Ramsgate: River Stour
Royal Tunbridge Wells: Court Lodge
  Down; Dunorland Park
Sandwich: River Stour; Stonar Lakes
Sevenoaks: Sundridge Lakes
Tonbridge: Gedges Lake

GAME FISHING
Lamberhurst: Bartley Mill Trout
  Fishery; Bewl Water

SEA FISHING
Broadstairs
Deal
Dover
Folkestone
Gravesend
Herne Bay
Hythe
Margate
Ramsgate
Shoreham-by-Sea
Whitstable

SURREY

COARSE FISHING
Dorking: Old Bury Hill Lake
Esher: River Thames
Farnham: River Thames
Godalming: River Thames
Guildford: River Thames
Haslemere: Great and Little Ponds
Leatherhead: River Thames
Reigate: Earlswood Common;
  Whitehall Farm
Sunbury: River Thames
Walton-on-Thames: River Thames
Weybridge: Leisure Sport Angling
Woking: River Thames

SUSSEX

COARSE FISHING
Alfriston: Seaford and Newhaven
  Angling Club
Arundel: Binstead Pond
Battle: Farthings Lake
Bexhill-on-Sea: Hastings and Bexhill
  Angling Club
Bodiam: River Rother

Chichester: Chichester Canal Society;
  Chichester and District Angling
  Society; Peckhams Copse
Crawley: Isfield Mill Pond; Tilgate Park
Crowborough: Crowborough & District
  Angling Association
Cuckfield: Ardingly College Pond;
  Ardingly Reservoir
Eastbourne: Compleat Angler Tackle
  Shop; Tony's Tackle Shop
East Grinstead: Fen Place Mill;
  Scarletts Lake; Weir Wood Reservoir
Hailsham: Cuckmere
Hastings: Clive Vale Reservoirs;
  Pevensey Levels
Haywards Heath: Ditchling Common
  Pond
Hove: River Adur; River Arun; Lagoon
  Tackle Shop
Petworth: Coultershaw Mill
Pevensey: Pevensey Levels
Rye: Pett Pools; Powdermill Water
Shoreham-by-Sea: River Darent
Winchelsea: Pett Pools

GAME FISHING
Arundel: Sussex County Angling
  Association; Chalk Springs Trout
  Fishery
Battle: Darwell and Powdermill Lakes
Bexhill-on-Sea: Hastings Fly Fishers
  Club Ltd
Chichester: Furnace Park Trout Fishery
Eastbourne: Arlington Reservoir
Horsham: Wattlehurst Lake

SEA FISHING
Bexhill-on-Sea
Brighton
Eastbourne
Hastings
Littlehampton
Newhaven
Worthing

Football

Football has always been a popular sport both to play and to watch. This popularity has reached unparalleled proportions in recent years with professional players reaching the status previously accorded only to stars of the screen or the pop world. Always colourful and often exciting the league teams are worth a visit one Saturday afternoon – you might well be watching a soccer star of the future in action!

Hove: Brighton and Hove Albion
    Football Club

Golf

Golf is a relaxing and increasingly popular sport for a wide range of people. The golf clubs listed welcome visitors but it is advisable that you contact the club in advance of playing in order to check if they have any restrictions – some require a handicap certificate or will only accept visitors who are members of another club. It is also worthwhile checking what the fees and hire charges are and what facilities are available. Most clubs have a pro-shop on the course where clubs and equipment can be hired and the professional will give tuition.

KENT

Ashford: Ashford (Kent) Golf Club
Biggin Hill: Addington Court Golf Courses; Cherry Lodge Golf Club; High Elms Golf Club
Broadstairs: North Foreland Golf Club
Bromley: Beckenham Place Park Golf Club; Bromley Golf Club; Chislehurst Golf Club; Magpie Hall Lane Municipal Golf Club; Shortlands Golf Club; Sidcup Golf Club; Sundridge Park Golf Club
Canterbury: Broome Park Golf and Country Club; Canterbury Golf Club
Chatham: Chatham Golf Centre
Dartford: Bexley Heath Golf Club; Dartford Golf Club Ltd
Deal: Royal Cinque Ports Golf Club
Edenbridge: Edenbridge Golf and Country Club
Folkestone: Sene Valley; Folkestone and Hythe Golf Club Ltd
Gillingham: Gillingham Golf Club Ltd
Gravesend: Mid Kent Golf Club
Herne Bay: Herne Bay Golf Club
Hythe: Hythe Imperial Golf Club
Lamberhurst: Lamberhurst Golf Club
Leeds: Leeds Castle Golf Course
Maidstone: Bearsted Golf Course; Cobtree Manor Park Golf Club; West Malling Golf Club
New Romney: Littlestone Golf Club
Rochester: Deangate Ridge Golf Club; Rochester and Cobham Park Golf Club
Sevenoaks: Knole Park
Whitstable: Chestfield Golf Club

Club; Kingswood Golf and Country Club; The Oaks Sports Centre; Walton Heath Golf Club; Woodcote Park Golf Club Ltd
Camberley: Camberley Heath Golf Club; Pennyhill Park Country Club
Caterham: North Downs Golf Club
Cobham: Fairmile Driving Range; Silvermore Golf Club
Dorking: Betchworth Park Golf Club; Dorking Golf Club
Epsom: Epsom Golf Club; Horton Park Country Park; RAC Country Club; Surbiton Golf Club
Esher: Moore Place Golf Course; Sandown Park Golf Course; Thames Ditton and Esher Golf Club
Farnham: Farnham Golf Club Ltd; Farnham Park Golf Course; Hankley Common Golf Club
Godalming: Bramley Golf Club; Gatton Manor Hotel and Golf Club; Shillinglee Park Golf Course; West Surrey Golf Club
Guildford: The Drift Golf and Leisure Club; Guildford Golf Club; Puttenham Golf Club
Haslemere: Hindhead Golf Club; Shillinglee Park Golf Club
Leatherhead: Effingham Golf Club; Leatherhead Golf Club
Lingfield: Lingfield Park Golf Club
Reigate: Redhill and Reigate Golf Club; Reigate Heath Golf Club
Sunbury: Lakeham Golf Club
Walton-on-Thames: Burhill Golf Club
Weybridge: Foxhills Country Club
Woking: Hoebridge Golf Course; Windlemere Golf Club

SURREY

Banstead: Banstead Downs Golf Club; Chipstead Golf Club Ltd; Coulsden Court Golf Club Ltd; Cuddington Golf

SUSSEX

Bexhill-on-Sea: Cooden Beach Golf Club; Highwoods Golf Club
Bognor Regis: Bognor Regis Golf Club

Brighton: Brighton and Hove Golf Club; Dyke Golf Club; East Brighton Golf Club; Hollingbury Park; Pyecombe Golf Club; Waterhall Golf Club
Chichester: Goodwood Golf Club; Selsey Golf Club
Crawley: Copthorne Golf Club; Cottesmore Golf Club; Tilgate Forest Golf Club
Crowborough: Crowborough Beacon Golf Club; Haywards Heath Golf Club
Eastbourne: Downs Golf Club; Royal Eastbourne Golf Club; Willingdon Golf Club

East Grinstead: Ashdown Forest Hotel and Golf Course; Holtye Golf Club; Royal Ashdown Forest Golf Club (Old Course); Royal Ashdown Forest (New Course)
Haywards Heath: Horam Park Golf Course
Horsham: Mannings Heath Golf Course
Hove: West Hove Golf Club
Lewes: Lewes Golf Club
Littlehampton: Littlehampton Golf Club
Newhaven: Peacehaven Golf Club
Petworth: Cowdray Park Country Club
Pulborough: West Sussex Golf Club
St Leonards: Beasport Park Golf Club
Uckfield: Piltdown Golf Club

Horse Racing

Horse racing is a sport enjoyed by many but riding is not always the way in which race lovers participate – watching and betting are very often the form their involvement takes. Surrey is home of Epsom, one of the best known racecourses in the world, and 'glorious Goodwood' in Sussex is renowned for its summer race season. A 'day at the races' can be enjoyed by all at any of the region's racecourses.

KENT

Folkestone: Folkestone Racecourse

SURREY

Epsom: Epsom Racecourse
Esher: Sandown Park Racecourse

Lingfield: Lingfield Park Racecourse
Sunbury: Kempton Park

SUSSEX

Arundel: Fontwell Park
Brighton: Brighton Racecourse
Chichester: Goodwood Racecourse

Horse Riding

Riding is a very popular pursuit in Britain and there are many riding schools and equestrian centres throughout this region offering a range of facilities from residential instructional holidays to basic instruction and horse and pony hire. Some centres specialise in trail riding and pony trekking, some place a greater emphasis on horse care and stable management whilst others provide courses on a variety of equestrian skills such as show jumping, cross country and side saddle. The range of facilities provided may include an indoor school, a dressage ring or a cross country course. To discover more about the schools and riding in general you should contact the British Horse Society, whose address is below. They will send you detailed information on request as well as a list of their many publications.

British Horse Society
British Equestrian Centre
Stoneleigh
Kenilworth
Warwickshire
☎ 0203 696697

KENT

Ashford: Blue Barn Equestrian Centre; Oathill Farm Riding Centre
Biggin Hill: Chavic Park Farm; Greenacres Riding School Ltd
Broadstairs: Ditchling Common Stud; St Stephen's College Riding School
Canterbury: Chaucer Riding and Livery Stables; Oathill Farm Riding Centre
Chatham: The Royal Engineers Saddle Club
Dartford: Eaglesfield Equestrian Centre
Faversham: Willows Farm Horse Centre
Folkestone: Coombe Wood Stables; Limes Farm Training Centre
Goudhurst: Bedgebury Riding Centre; Lynx Park
Gravesend: Tollgate Stables
Hythe: Hayne Barn Riding School
Maidstone: Horseshoes Riding School; Lower Bell Riding School
Minster-in-Sheppey: Taylor's Riding Establishment
Ramsgate: Nelson Park Riding Centre; Taylor's Riding Establishment
Sevenoaks: Bradbourne Riding and Training Centre Ltd; Chelsfield Riding School; Eaglesfield Equestrian Centre
Sissinghurst: Appletree Stables
Tenterden: Moat House; Nelson Park Riding Centre
Tonbridge: Riding Farm

SURREY

Banstead: The Clock Tower Riding Centre; Farthing Down Stables; Huntersfield Farm Riding Centre; Orchard Cottage Riding Stables; Wildwoods Riding Centre
Caterham: Beechwood Riding School; Woldingham Equestrian Centre
Cobham: Cobham Manor Riding Centre; Lower Farm Riding and Livery Stables
Dorking: Dorking Riding School; Parkhurst Horse Training Facilities; Partridge Stables
Epsom: Headley Grove Riding and Livery Stables Ltd
Esher: South Weylands Equestrian Centre
Farnham: Old Park Stables; Priory School of Equitation
Godalming: Greenways Farm and Stables
Haslemere: Grangefield Children's Riding School; Southern Equitation Livery Centre
Leatherhead: Vale Lodge Stables
Lingfield: Little Brook Equestrian Centre; Oldencraig Equestrian Centre
Reigate: Orchard Cottage Riding Stables
Walton-on-Thames: South Weylands Equestrian Centre
Woking: Langshot Equestrian Centre

SUSSEX

Alfriston: Winton Street Farm Stables
Arundel: Arundel Riding Centre
Chichester: Zara Stud and Training Centres
East Grinstead: Belmoredean Stud and Livery Stables
Hastings: Higham Farm

Heathfield: Sky Farm Riding School
Horley: Burstow Park Riding and Livery Centre
Horsham: Naldretts Farm
Lewes: Crockstead Equestrian Centre
Polegate: Cophall Farm Stables; Gatewood Stables
Pulborough: Coldwaltham House; West Sussex College of Agriculture and Horticulture
Seaford: Gatewood Stables
Steyning: West Wolves Riding Centre
Uckfield: Canters End Riding School
Winchelsea: Higham Farm

Orienteering

Orienteering is a wonderful way to get out into the countryside no matter what your age or level of fitness. You can run, jog or walk as you read your map and choose your route to the red and white markers. You can go solo or share your experiences with friends and family – there's a course for everyone and groups of two and four are welcome on beginners courses. It costs very little and you can try it out at one of the permanent orienteering courses. If you like maps, fresh air and exploring the countryside then this could be the leisure activity for you. The British Orienteering Federation, whose address is below, will supply you with details of clubs and future events as well as a list of the permanent orienteering courses around the country.

British Orienteering Federation
Riversdale
Dale Road North
Darley Dale
Matlock
Derbyshire
☎ 0269 673042

KENT

Gravesend: Shorne Wood Country Park
Rochester: Arethusa Venture Centre

Tennis

Britain might not have produced a top-class tennis player in recent years but that cannot be attributed to lack of facilities. There are excellent indoor and outdoor courts, floodlit all-weather courts and expert tuition is also available. Complete beginners to experienced players concentrating on advanced techniques are catered for by the professional coaches in some of the coaching programmes. There are public tennis courts, usually hard, in most parks, recreation areas and leisure centres. You can hire them for a small fee and only have to turn up to play.

For anyone interested in lawn tennis the Lawn Tennis Association will supply you with information about their clubs and play opportunities if you approach them at the address given below.

Lawn Tennis Association
J C U James (Secretary)
The Queen's Club
West Kensington
London
☎ 071 385 2366

KENT

Broadstairs: Memorial Recreation Ground
Bromley: Bromley Sports Hall
Folkestone: Folkestone Sports Centre
Gravesend: Record Tennis Centre
Hythe: Record Tennis Centre
Maidstone: Record Tennis Centre; Westborough Sports Centre
Margate: Hartsdown Park
Northfleet: Wombwell Park
Ramsgate: Montefiore Avenue; Warre Recreation Ground
Rochester: Jacksons Recreation Ground
Sevenoaks: Hollybush Lane Recreation Ground

SURREY

Banstead: Transworld Tennis
Dorking: Dorking Lawn Tennis and Squash Club
Woking: Chris Lane Tennis Centre

SUSSEX

Bexhill-on-Sea: Bexhill Tennis Centre
Crawley: Crawley Leisure Centre; Langley Green Playing Fields; Southgate Playing Fields
Crowborough: Crowborough Tennis and Squash Club; Wolfe Recreation Ground
Eastbourne: Cavendish Sports Centre; The Ball Park
Hastings: Alexandra Park
Horsham: Park Recreation Centre; Weald Recreation Centre
Hove: Record Tennis Centre
Littlehampton: Maltravers Leisure Park; The Sportsground
Newhaven: Tideway Leisure Centre

27

Walking & Rambling

Walking, rambling or, perhaps ambling will provide everyone, no matter what their age, with the opportunity to discover the charms of the countryside and the country inns that provide ideal stopping places for refreshments. The pace is entirely up to the walker and the route could be one selected from the OS map or one suggested in one of the innumerable books and leaflets of walks and nature trails. Many popular routes are signposted and footpaths, byways and bridlepaths have been linked in certain areas to form long distance routes which are well marked and easy to follow. The local Tourist Information Centres usually have a good selection of leaflets on local walks and if you would like to join a planned programme of walks the Ramblers' Association will provide you with details of their activities and club walks. The Long Distance Walkers Association will provide OS maps and guidebooks for recommended walks on request.

The Ramblers' Association
1/5 Wandsworth Road
London
☎ 071 582 6878

Long Distance Walkers Association
Mr P Dyson (Secretary)
30 Park Avenue
Roundhay
Leeds
West Yorkshire
☎ 0532 657029

KENT

Bromley: Cuckoo Wood Trail; Jubilee Country Park; The Nash Circular Walk; West Wickham Town and Country Walk
Canterbury: North Downs Way
Dartford: Darent Valley Path; Dartford Heath
Dover: North Downs Way
Dymchurch: Romney Marsh Walks

Faversham: A Walk Around Faversham; Perry Wood; Saxon Shore Way
Folkestone: The Warren
Gillingham: Riverside Country Park; Saxon Shore Way
Gravesend: Cobham Walks; Gordon Memorial Walk; Gravesham; Dickens Country; Saxon Shore Way; The Weald Way
Lydd: Romney Marsh Walks
Maidstone: Haysden Country Park; A Walk around Maidstone
Rochester: A Walk Around the City; North Downs Way
Royal Tunbridge Wells: A Circular Promenade; Cumberland Walk
Sevenoaks: Sevenoaks Group Ramblers' Association

SUSSEX

Alfriston: South Downs Way
Battle: Rother Walks

Burgess Hill: Ramblers' Association
Crawley: Worth Way
Crowborough: High Weald Walkers
Eastbourne: The Weald Way
Hastings: Hastings Country Park
Littlehampton: History Trail; Clymping Circular Walk
Polegate: The Arlington Bluebell Walk
Seaford: Seven Sisters Country Park

SURREY

Dorking: Box Hill
Epsom: Horton Country Park
Esher: Woodland and Heathland Walks
Farnham: North Downs Way
Haslemere: Devil's Jumps; Hindhead, Invalland and Weydown Commons
Reigate: Earlswood Common; Redhill Common; Reigate Heath

Special Interests

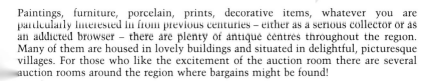

Antiques

Paintings, furniture, porcelain, prints, decorative items, whatever you are particularly interested in from previous centuries – either as a serious collector or as an addicted browser – there are plenty of antique centres throughout the region. Many of them are housed in lovely buildings and situated in delightful, picturesque villages. For those who like the excitement of the auction room there are several auction rooms around the region where bargains might be found!

KENT

Bromley: Antica
Canterbury: Acorn Antiques
Chilham: Chilham Square

SURREY

Banstead: Carshalton Antique Gallery
Camberley: The Antique House
Farnham: Farnham Antiques Centre

SUSSEX

Arundel: Arundel Bridge Antiques
Brighton: The Lanes
Chichester: Bosham Antiques
Crawley: Hickmet Southways Ltd
Eastbourne: Douglas Barnsley
Hastings: Maheen Hevduk Antiques
Lewes: Pastorale Antiques; Young Lionel Antiques
Littlehampton: Joan's Antiques

Aquariums

For the lovers of the 'deep' there are sea-life centres where it is possible to experience the unique magic of the underwater world with deep-sea creatures only inches away. You can see dolphins, sharks, turtles and seals at Brighton or walk through the underground aquarium at Eastbourne.

SURREY

Farnham: Underwaterworld

SUSSEX

Brighton: Brighton Aquarium and
Dolphinarium

Eastbourne: Redoubt Fortress Aquarium
Hastings: Sea Life Centre

Art Galleries

This region has some very distinguished galleries with internationally renowned collections of famous artists as well as several smaller galleries displaying the work of local artists many of whom have been inspired by the sea and its craft.

KENT

Ashford: Evegate Farm Art Gallery
Canterbury: The Graphics Gallery; Royal Museum, Art Gallery and Buffs Regimental Museum
Hythe: Port Lympne House
Maidstone: Maidstone Museum and Art Gallery
Royal Tunbridge Wells: Tunbridge Wells Museum and Art Gallery
Westerham: Squerryes Court

SURREY

Dorking: Gomshall Mill & Gallery; Westcott Gallery
Farnham: New Ashgate Gallery; West Surrey College of Art & Design
Guildford: Guildford House Gallery; University of Surrey Library Gallery; The Watts Gallery
Horley: Outwood Art Gallery and Sculpture Park

SUSSEX

Arundel: Arundel Castle; River Gallery
Brighton: Brighton Museum and Art Gallery; Gardener Theatre; Rottingdean Grange Art Gallery and Museum
Eastbourne: Toner Art Gallery and Local History Museum
Hastings: Hastings Museum and Art Gallery
Horsham: Lennards Gallery
Hove: Hove Museum and Art Gallery
Lewes: Bentley Wildfowl and Motor Museum; Firle Place
Littlehampton: Littlehampton Maritime Museum
Petworth: Petworth House
Rye: Rye Art Gallery
St Leonards: Photogallery
Worthing: Worthing Museum and Art Gallery

Arts & Crafts

Arts and crafts are richly represented in this area from hand-painted silk to decorated-style earthenware produced to 17th century designs, model museums to woodcraft. There is an unusual three-acre site with over 2000 different Philippine handicrafts in Kent; the centre is soon to expand to include a three acre site of British handicrafts as well.

KENT

Canterbury: Summer Academy
Dartford: David Evans and Company
Lamberhurst: Mr Heaver's Noted Model Museum and Craft Village; Hook Green Pottery

Leeds: Kent Garden Costume Dolls
Maidstone: Mill Yard Craft Centre; Whitbread Hop Farm Craft Centre
New Romney: Philippine Craft Centre
Sittingbourne: Oad Street Craft Centre

SURREY

Dorking: The Hannah Peschar Gallery
Epsom: Horton Park Farm
Farnham: Manor Farm Craft Centre
Godalming: Mary Wondrausch;
Thursley Textile Designs
Haslemere: Grayshott Pottery

SUSSEX

Alfriston: Drusillas Park
Arundel: The Arundel Fine Glass &
Engraving Studio
Bodiam: The Craftsman Gallery Pottery
Workshop
Chichester: Bosham Walk; Geraldine
St Aubyn Hubbard
Hailsham: The Truggery
Lewes: The Old Needlemakers; Mary
Potter Studio
Shoreham-by-Sea: Henfield Woodcraft
Worthing: Smugglers Annex

Country Parks

There has been a steadily growing awareness of the importance of retaining areas of
countryside for recreational use and this has led to the designation of many areas of
ancient and new woodland, downland, lakes, parkland and heathland as country
parks. Ranging in size from under five to hundreds of acres, they offer country walks,
fishing, horse rides, sailing, water sports, picnicking and nature reserves – plenty for
everyone to enjoy.

KENT

Bromley: Chislehurst Common; Crystal
Palace Park; High Elms Estate;
Jubilee Country Park; Petts Wood
Gillingham: Riverside Country Park
Gravesend: Shorne Wood
Herne Bay: Reculver Country Park
Lamberhurst: Bewl Water
Maidstone: Cobtree Manor Park; Mote
Park
Tonbridge: Haysden Country Park

SURREY

Banstead: The Banstead Commons;
North Park
Camberley: Lightwater Country Park
Dorking: Box Hill
Epsom: Horton Country Park
Haslemere: Frensham Common

SUSSEX

Bexhill-on-Sea: Broad Oak Country
Park
Crawley: Buchan Country Park; Tilgate
Park
Crowborough: Jarvis Brook Country
Park

Hastings: Hastings Country Park
Horsham: Buchan Country Park;
Southwater Country Park
Seaford: Seven Sisters Country Park
Uckfield: Wilderness Wood

Factory Tours

The processes involved in the production of many well-known objects, both large and small, are fascinating to see. Some factories allow visitors to tour and see the stages involved in the manufacture of the finished item. Enjoy watching and perhaps tasting the stages in cider and wine-making, there are several large vineyards and a well known cider producer in this area.

KENT

Leeds: Kent Garden Costume Dolls;
  Kent Garden Vineyard
Maidstone: Whitbread Hop Farm Craft
  Centre

SUSSEX

Battle: Carr Taylor Vineyards
Heathfield: Merrydown Cider
Petworth: Lurgashall Winery

Farm Parks

Farm Parks will allow you to spend 'a day down on the farm' and see the farm at work. You can watch the cows being milked and the milk being pasteurised and bottled, see the calves, pigs and chickens and rare breeds of domestic animals, or wander around collections of farm machinery and horse-drawn waggons – a wonderful way to see the countryside in action.

KENT

Canterbury: Parsonage Farm Rural
  Heritage Centre
Dartford: Stone Lodge Farm Park
Maidstone: Whitbread Hop Farm
New Romney: Dunrobin Stud
Sevenoaks: Great Hollanden Farm
Sittingbourne: Gore Farm
Tonbridge: Badsell Park Farm

SURREY

Caterham: Godstone Farm
Dorking: Chapel Farm Animal Trail
Epsom: Horton Park Farm
Guildford: Loseley Park Farm; The Old
  Farm at Shere

SUSSEX

Eastbourne: Seven Sisters Sheep Centre
Haywards Heath: Burstye Soays
Petworth: Noah's Farmyard

Rye: The Children's Farm
Uckfield: Ashdown Forest Farm;
  Heaven Farm; Ketches Friendly
  Animal Farm

33

Festivals & Fairs

The customs, traditions and history of the area live through the festivals and fairs that make the whole region a colourful, lively and fascinating world through the seasons. Everywhere are flower festivals, fairs, literature festivals, gymkhanas, regattas, and music festivals. Many of the smaller events are more than worth a detour and a visit. They reveal much about the villages and towns that foster them and there are several events in this region, the Glyndebourne Festival or the Brighton Veteran Car Rally, for example, that draw international support and acclaim.

KENT

Broadstairs: Dickens Festival; Carnival; Folk Week; Water Gala

Dickens Festival, Broadstairs

Bromley: St Giles' Fair
Canterbury: Chaucer Festival; Cricket Week; Arts Festival; Carol Service
Deal: Music Festival
Dymchurch: Dr Syn Carnival
Folkestone: International Folklore Festival; Kent Literature Festival
Gillingham: International Showjumping; Arts Festival; Water Festival
Gravesend: Gravesham Riverside Fair; Summer Regatta
Leeds: Leeds Castle Fireworks
Maidstone: International Balloon Festival; Maidstone Carnival; Maidstone River Festival; Maidstone Festival; Maidstone Beer Festival; North Kent Festival of Cultures
Northfleet: Northfleet Carnival
Ramsgate: Ramsgate Royal Harbour Heritage Festival
Rochester: Dickens Festival; River Festival; Norman Rochester; Dickensian Christmas
Sevenoaks: Summer Festival; Cricket Week; Riverhead Carnival
Whitstable: Blessing of the Waters; Oyster Festival; Whitstable Regatta; Carnival

SURREY

Dorking: Box Hill Music Festival
Epsom: Derby Day
Guildford: Dicing for Maid's Money; County Show; Guildford Festival
Haslemere: Music Festival
Sunbury: Gala Evening; Christmas Festival

SUSSEX

Arundel: Corpus Christi Flowers and Floral Festival; Arundel Festival
Battle: Marbles Match; Music and Drama Festival; Bonfire and Torchlight Procession
Bexhill-on-Sea: Horse Show; Music Festival
Bognor Regis: International Clown Convention; Carnival Week; International Birdman Rally
Brighton: Festival on Ice; British Craft and Arts Fair; Brighton International Festival; Old Ship Royal Escape Yacht Race; London to Brighton RAC Veteran Car Run
Chichester: Music Festival; Chichester Gala; Chichester Festivities; Glorious Goodwood; Royal Military Police March; Goodwood National Dressage
Eastbourne: Folk Festival; Women's International Folk Festival
Glynde: Glyndebourne Festival Opera
Hastings: Chess Congress; Musical Festival; Blessing the Sea; Hastings Week
Lewes: Bonfire Celebrations
Littlehampton: Littlehampton Carnival
St Leonards: National Town Criers' Championship
Worthing: Seafront Fayre

Food & Drink

The rich soils and mild climate of this region have produced a variety of delicious produce. Kent is known as the 'garden of England'. Its orchards and vineyards produce top-quality fruits and there are award-winning vineyards with excellent English wines to try as well as some delicious ciders. For a taste of the sea look no further than Whitstable, it is renowned for its oysters.

KENT

Ashford: Headcorn Flowers and Vineyard
Canterbury: Breach, Barham; Elham Valley Vineyards; St Nicholas of Ash Vineyard and Winery; Theobalds Barn Cider
Edenbridge: Chiddingstone Vineyards Ltd
Faversham: Shepherd Neame Brewery
Lamberhurst: Lamberhurst Vineyard; The Weald Smokery
Maidstone: Bearsted Vineyard; Headcorn Vineyard
Royal Tunbridge Wells: Penshurst Vineyards
Sittingbourne: Syndale Valley Vineyards
Tenterden: Harbourne Vineyard; Tenterden Vineyards
Whitstable: Oysters

SURREY

Guildford: Loseley Dairy Produce

SUSSEX

Alfriston: The English Wine Centre
Arundel: Arundel Vineyards
Battle: Carr Taylor Vineyards
Bodiam: Seddlescombe Vineyard
Chichester: Chilsdown Vineyard
Crowborough: Castle Hill Farm
Eastbourne: Seven Sisters Sheep Centre
Heathfield: Merrydown Cider; St George's Vineyard
Petworth: Lurgashall Winery
Pulborough: Nutbourne Manor Vineyard
Uckfield: Barkham Manor Vineyard; Flexerne Vineyard

Kentish Oast Houses

Forest Parks

Ancient and newly created woodland areas throughout this region are open to walk through and enjoy. There are nature trails, conservation centres and other interesting features for the visitor to explore. Ashdown Forest is immortalised in the map of 'Pooh country' – perhaps you will find a stream to play 'poohsticks' in!

KENT

Herne Bay: Wealden Forest Park

SURREY

Farnham: Alice Holt Forest Visitor Centre

SUSSEX

Crowborough: Ashdown Forest

Fun Parks

Whether it's waltzers, roller coasters, dodgems or big wheels the coastal resorts offer all the fun of the fair at their permanent fun park sites. There are rides for the very young and amusements for the not-so-young too – entertainment for all the family.

KENT

Dymchurch: Feathers
Folkestone: Rotunda Amusement Park

SUSSEX

Bognor Regis: Rainbow's End Circus World; Butlin's Southcoast World
Hastings: Jungle Tumble; Pleasure Island
Littlehampton: Smarts Amusement Park
Worthing: Brooklands; The Lido

Gardens

Whether on a grand scale and landscaped by Capability Brown or tiny cottage gardens created by the love of successive inhabitants over the years, gardens are always places to inspire and revive the most weary of spirits. A constant tribute to the co-operation of man and nature, a natural painting using the richest possible palette, one that changes with the seasons, gardens satisfy all the senses whilst also harbouring a glorious array of wildlife. Kent, Surrey and Sussex have many beautiful gardens, formal and grand, intricate and herbal, rambling and fragrant, open for you to explore.

KENT

Ashford: Godinton House Gardens
Bromley: The Maze
Canterbury: Gooderston Park
Chilham: Chilham Castle Gardens
Dartford: St John's Jerusalem Garden

Deal: Northbourne Court Garden
Dover: The Pines Garden
Edenbridge: Hever Castle Gardens
Faversham: Doddington Place Gardens;
    Mount Ephraim Gardens

Goudhurst: Bedgebury National Pinetum
Gravesend: Camer Park; Cobham Hall
Hythe: Port Lympne House
Lamberhurst: Emmets; Scotney Castle Gardens; Sprivers Gardens
Leeds: Leeds Castle
Royal Tunbridge Wells: Owl House Gardens; Penshurst Place
Sevenoaks: Great Comp Garden; Knole; Riverhill House Gardens
Sissinghurst: Sissinghurst Castle Garden
Tonbridge: Tonbridge Castle Grounds
Walmer: Walmer Castle Gardens
Westerham: Chartwell

SURREY

Cobham: Painshill Park
Dorking: Polseden Lacey
Esher: Claremont Landscape Gardens
Farnham: Old Kiln Museum
Godalming: Busbridge Lakes; Winkworth Arboretum
Reigate: Castle Grounds; Priory Park
Sunbury: The Walled Garden
Virginia Water: Savill Gardens; Valley Gardens

Woking: The Royal Horticultural Society's Garden

SUSSEX

Arundel: Denmans Gardens
Bodiam: Haremere Hall; Great Dixter House and Gardens
Chichester: Apuldram Roses; Earnley Butterflies and Gardens; West Dean Gardens
Crawley: Nymans Garden
Crowborough: Borde Hill Garden; Leigh Manor
Eastbourne: Motcombe Park
Hailsham: Michelham Priory
Haywards Heath: Borde Hill Garden; Wakehurst Place Gardens
Horsham: Leonardslee Gardens
Lewes: Southover Grange Gardens
Newhaven: Tate's Garden Paradise
Petworth: Petworth House Gardens
Pulborough: Parham House Gardens
Rye: Brickwall; Great Dixter
Uckfield: Sheffield Park Garden
Worthing: Highdown Gardens

Guided Tours

There are many experts to show you the delights of the south-east. The major cities and towns in this region support Registered Guides who will have attended a training course sponsored by the various Tourist Boards, they can be identified by the 'Blue Badge' they wear. Some of these regional guides also have a regional endorsement; enquire when you are making your booking. Several of the individual historic houses, churches and museums offer their own guided tours; they will give full details of times and duration of tours on application. The Tourist Board will provide information sheets on guided activities which are available from the address below.

South East England Tourist Board
The Old Brew House, Warwick Park
Tunbridge Wells
☎ 0892 540766

KENT

Canterbury: Canterbury Guild of Guides
Deal: Town Trail
Faversham: Stone Chapel
Sevenoaks: Trust Tours

SURREY

Guildford: Town Tours

SUSSEX

Arundel: Mary Godby
Chichester: Tourist Information Centre
Hastings: Old Town Walks; Sightseeing Tours
St Leonards: Burton's St Leonards Society
Steyning: West Sussex History Tours

Heritage

Over the centuries waves of invaders have entered England through its south-eastern corner. There are ruins of numerous Roman shore castles some of which have been incorporated into mediaeval castles. The Anglo-Saxons have left their mark as have the Danes – the Cinque Ports were established to repel them. The Norman invasion led to a period rich in history and left many legacies including the great fortresses that can be found at Canterbury, Dover and Rochester. The region's ecclesiastical heritage is reflected in its abbeys. The first Cistercian Abbey in England, founded in the first century, is in Surrey.

Rochester Castle

KENT

Bromley: Caesar's Well; Chislehurst Caves
Canterbury: St Augustine's Abbey
Chilham: Julieberrie's Grave
Deal: Sandown Castle
Dover: Grand Shaft; The Pharos
Faversham: Stone Chapel
Folkestone: Sandgate Castle
Herne Bay: Reculver Towers and Roman Fort
Lamberhurst: Bayham Abbey; Old Soar Manor; Scotney Castle
Leeds: Sutton Valence Castle
Lullingstone: Eynsford Castle; Lullingstone Roman Villa
Maidstone: Kits Coty; St Leonard's Tower
Margate: Margate Caves

Royal Tunbridge Wells: Bayham Abbey; Eynford Castle; St Leonard's Tower
Tonbridge: Tonbridge Castle
Westerham: Hever Castle

SURREY

Chertsey: Runnymede
Farnham: Farnham Castle Keep; Waverley Abbey
Guildford: Guildford Castle

SUSSEX

Alfriston: Long Man of Wilmington
Brighton: Devil's Dyke
Chichester: City Walls; Fishbourne Roman Palace and Museum
Hastings: Hastings Castle
Lewes: Lewes Castle
Pevensey: Pevensey Castle
Rye: Landgate

Historic Buildings

The buildings of the south-east reflect the different influences that have affected the area over the centuries. The region's ecclesiastical past can be seen in the magnificent cathedrals at Chichester and Canterbury. The cathedral at Canterbury reflects its importance as the Mother Church of Anglicans throughout the world. The landscape of the south-east features many unusual buildings such as the Martello Towers, built as a coastal defence against Napoleon, and the characteristically Kentish oast houses. The exotic and the flamboyant can be seen in Brighton where the Royal Pavilion adds its distinctive silhouette to this coastal town's skyline.

Canterbury Cathedral

KENT

Broadstairs: North Foreland Lighthouse; Crompton Tower; The Pavilion; St Peter's Church; York Gate

Bromley: Bromley College; The Free Watermen's and Lightermen's Almshouses; St Giles the Abbot Parish Church; St John's Parish Church; The Priory; The Rawlins Almshouses; Seadbury Estate

Canterbury: Canterbury Cathedral; Poor Priests Hospital

Chilham: Chilham Castle

Dartford: St Margarets Church; Wat Tyler Public House

Deal: Deal Castle

Dover: Crabble Corn Mill; Dover Castle; St Edmund's Chapel; St Mary-in-Castro Church

Dungeness: Dungeness Lighthouse

Edenbridge: Chiddingstone Castle; Haxted Watermill and Museum; Hever Castle

Faversham: Abbey Street; Chart Gunpowder Mills

Folkestone: St Mary and Eanswythe Church

Gillingham: St Mary Magdalene Church

Gravesend: Cobham College; Meopham Windmill; Milton Chantry; New Tavern Fort; The Leather Bottle Inn; St George's Church; The Old Forge; St Mary's Church

Herne Bay: Herne Windmill

Hythe: Lympne Castle

Lamberhurst: Bartley Mill

Leeds: Leeds Castle

Lydd: All Saints Church

Margate: Drapers Mill; Salmestone Grange; Sarre Windmill; Shell Grotto

Minster-in-Sheppey: Harty Church; St Mary and Sexburga; Minster Abbey

New Romney: Newchurch Church; New Romney Church; Old Romney Church; Snave Church

Northfleet: Our Lady of the Assumption; St Botolphs
Ramsgate: St Augustine's Church
Rochester: Fort Amherst; Rochester Castle; Rochester Cathedral; Temple Manor; Upnor Castle
Royal Tunbridge Wells: King Charles the Martyr
Sandwich: White Mill Folk Museum; Richborough Castle
Tenterden: All Saints Church; Horne Palace Chapel; Stocks Mill; Woodchurch Windmill
Walmer: Walmer Castle

SURREY

Banstead: All Saints Church
Cobham: Chatley Heath Semaphore Tower; Church Stile House; St Mary Magdalene Church
Dorking: Leith Hill Tower; Polesden Lacey
Godalming: The Old Town Hall; Oakhurst Cottage; St Peter and St Paul
Guildford: Abbots Hospital; Guildford Cathedral; The Guildhall; Holy Trinity Church; Irvingite Church; Royal Grammar School; Shalford Mill; Watts Mortuary Chapel
Horley: The Post Mill
Leatherhead: St Mary & St Nicholas; St Nicholas' Church

Maidstone: Allington Castle; All Saints' Church; Archbishop's Palace; The Friars
Reigate: Reigate Castle; Reigate Priory; Church of St Mary Magdalene; Old Town Hall; Reigate Tunnel; The Windmill Church

SUSSEX

Alfriston: Lullington Church; St Andrews Church
Arundel: Arundel Castle; Arundel Cathedral
Battle: Battle Abbey; St Mary's
Bodiam: Bodiam Castle
Brighton: Royal Pavilion
Burwash: Mad Jack Fuller's Mausoleum
Chichester: Bishops Palace; Chichester Cathedral; St Mary's Hospital
Crawley: Isfield Mill
East Grinstead: High Street; Old Place; Sackville College; St Augustine's Church
Glynde: Glynde Place
Hailsham: Church of St Mary the Virgin; Herstmonceux Castle; Horselunger Manor; Michelham Priory
Haywards Heath: St Peter's Church
Hove: West Blatchington Windmill
Lewes: Firle Place; Monks House
Newhaven: Newhaven Fort
Rye: Camber Castle
Worthing: High Salvingdon Windmill

Leeds Castle

Historic Houses

Over the centuries the fortunes of the country affected those of the regions and in turn were reflected in the style and grandeur of the houses built. Some included in this guide were the site of an historic event or the dwelling of a famous figure, others represent a family's prestige and a style of architecture. Most exhibit levels of workmanship and decoration that can be marvelled at and appreciated by all who see them.

KENT

Ashford: Godinton House
Broadstairs: Bleak House
Bromley: Camden Place; Down House; The Palace; Sundridge Park
Dartford: St John's Jerusalem
Faversham: Belmont
Goudhurst: Finchcocks
Gravesend: Cobham Hall; Gads Hill Place; Owletts
Hythe: Port Lympne House
Lullingstone: Lullingstone Castle
Maidstone: Boughton Monchelsea Place; Stoneacre
Margate: Quex House and Gardens
Royal Tunbridge Wells: Penshurst Place
Sevenoaks: Ightham Mote; Knole
Sissinghurst: Sissinghurst Castle
Tenterden: Smallhythe Place
Westerham: Chartwell; Quebec House; Squerryes Court

SURREY

Guildford: Albury Park; Loseley House
Lingfield: Great Manor

SUSSEX

Alfriston: Charleston Farmhouse; The Old Clergy House
Bodiam: Great Dixter House and Gardens; Haremere Hall
Bognor Regis: Hotham House
Brighton: Preston Manor
Chichester: Goodwood House; Pallant House
East Grinstead: Hammerwood House; Priest House; Standen
Petworth: Petworth House
Pulborough: Parham House
Rye: Brickwall House; Lamb House
Steyning: Chantry Green House; St Mary's House

Bleak House, Broadstairs

Museums

There are museums covering such diverse interests as shops, shipwrecks, toys, agricultural bygones or vintage vehicles. Some record purely local history whilst others such as the Dickens Centre in Rochester and the Dog Collar Museum at Leeds Castle cover more specific topics! Whatever you might have a particular fascination for, there is probably a museum in this region to broaden your knowledge and feed your interest in the subject.

Old Town Gaol, Dover

KENT

Ashford: Local History Museum; Wye College Agricultural Museum

Broadstairs: Crampton Tower Museum; Dickens House Museum

Bromley: Bromley Museum; Down House; The Priory

Canterbury: Canterbury Centre; Canterbury Heritage Museum; Canterbury Pilgrims Way; Ethnic Doll and Toy Museum; Royal Museum; Art Gallery and Buffs Regimental Museum; St Augustine's Abbey; West Gate Museum

Chatham: Fort Amherst; Old Brook Pumping Station; The Historic Dockyard

Dartford: Dartford Borough Museum

Deal: Costume and Accessories Museum; Deal Archaeological Collection; Deal Castle; Maritime and Local History Museum; Time-Ball Tower; Victoriana Museum

Dover: Dover Museum; Dover Transport Museum; Frontline Dover; Maison Dieu; The Bay Museum; The Roman Painted House; Old Town Gaol

Dungeness: Martello Tower 24

Edenbridge: Haxted Watermill and Museum; Hever Castle

Faversham: Belmont; Chart Gunpowder Mills; Fleur de Lis Heritage Centre; Maison Dieu Heritage Museum

Folkestone: Eurotunnel Exhibition Centre; Folkestone Museum and Art Gallery; Kent Battle of Britain Museum

Gillingham: Royal Engineers Museum; Urban Heritage Centre

Goudhurst: Finchcocks

Gravesend: Gravesham Museum

Herne Bay: Herne Bay Museum

Hythe: Hythe Local History Room; Lympne Castle; Port Lympne House

Lamberhurst: Mr Heaver's Noted Model Museum and Craft Village

Leeds: Dog Collar Museum

Maidstone: Maidstone Museum and Art Gallery; Museum of Kent Rural Life; Museum of the Queen's Own Royal West Kent Regiment; Tyrwhitt-Drake Museum of Carriages; Whitbread Hop Farm

Margate: Old Town Hall Local History Museum; Powell Cotton Museum; Quex House Museum; Tudor House and Museum

Minster: Minster Abbey and Gatehouse Museum

Northfleet: Blue Circle Heritage Centre

Ramsgate: East Kent Maritime Museum; Ramsgate Museum; Maritime Museum; Motor Museum; Agricultural and Rural Life Museum

Rochester: The Dickens Centre; Guildhall Museum; Kenneth Bills Rochester Motorcycle Museum; Six Poor Travellers House

Royal Tunbridge Wells: A Day at the Wells; David Salomon's House; Penshurst Place; Tunbridge Wells Museum and Art Gallery

Sandwich: The Precinct Toy Museum; Sandwich Guildhall and Museum; White Mill Folk Museum

Sevenoaks: Sevenoaks Museum

Sheerness: Battle of Britain Lace Panel; Rose Street Heritage Centre

Sissinghurst: Brattle Farm Museum

Sittingbourne: Bradbury House Victorian Museum; Old Court Hall Museum; Dolphin Yard Sailing Barge Museum

Steyning: National Butterfly Museum

Tenterden: Smallhythe Place; Stocks Mill; Tenterden and District Museum

Whitstable: Whitstable Museum

SURREY

Camberley: Royal Army Ordnance Corps Museum

Caterham: East Surrey Museum

Chertsey: Chertsey Museum

Cobham: Cobham Bus Museum

Egham: Egham Museum

Farnham: Farnham Museum; Old Kiln Museum

Godalming: Godalming Museum

Guildford: Guildford Museum; Hatchlands; Shere Museum; Womens Royal Army Corps Museum

Horley: The Post Mill

Leatherhead: Fire and Iron Gallery; Leatherhead Museum of Local History

Reigate: Reigate and Banstead Heritage Centre; Reigate Priory Museum

Weybridge: Brooklands Museum; Weybridge Museum

SUSSEX

Alfriston: Alfriston Heritage Centre and Blacksmiths Museum; Wilmington Priory

Arundel: Amberley Chalk Pits Museum; Arundel Museum and Heritage Centre; Arundel Toy and Military Museum

Battle: Battle Museum; Buckley's Museum of Shops

Bexhill-on-Sea: Bexhill Museum; Bexhill Museum of Costume and Social History

Bodiam: Ditchling Museum; Quarry Steam Centre

Bognor Regis: Bognor Regis Local History Museum

Brighton: The Barlow Collection; Booth Museum of Natural History; Brighton Museum and Art Gallery; National Museum of Penny Slot Machines; Rottingdean Grange Art Gallery and Museum

Chichester: Chichester District Museum; Fishbourne Roman Palace and Museum; Guidhall Museum; Mechanical Music and Doll Collection; Museum of D-Day Aviation; The Red Cap Museum; Tangmere Military Aviation Museum; Weald and Downland Open Air Museum

Crowborough: Conan Doyle (Crowborough) Establishment

Eastbourne: Eastbourne Heritage Centre; How We Lived Then Museum; Lifeboat Museum; Martello Tower 73; The Redoubt Fortress; Towner Art Gallery and Local History Museum

East Grinstead: Priest House Museum

Hailsham: Heritage Centre; Michelham Priory

Hastings: Fishermens Museum; Hastings Domesday Exhibition; Hastings Embroidery; Hastings Museum and Art Gallery; Hastings Museum of Local History; Shipwreck Heritage Centre

Heathfield: Sussex Farm Museum

Horsham: Horsham Museum

Hove: Hove Museum and Art Gallery; The British Engineerium; West Blatchington Windmill

Lewes: Anne of Cleves House Museum; Bentley Wildfowl and Motor Museum; Lewes Living History Model; Military Heritage Museum; Museum of Sussex Archaeology

Littlehampton: Littlehampton Maritime Museum

Newhaven: Newhaven Fort

Petworth: Lurgashall Winery

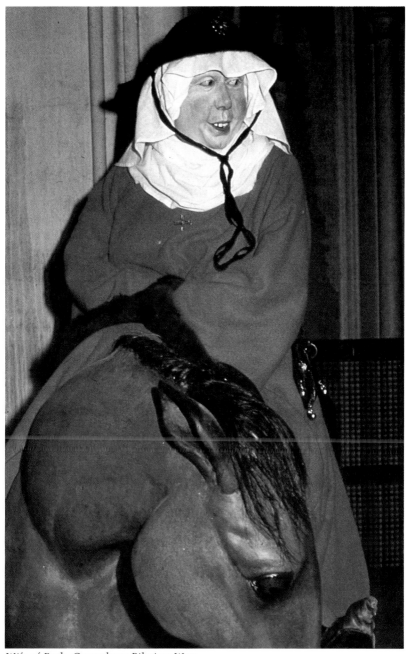

Wife of Bath, Canterbury Pilgrims Way

Polegate: Filching Manor Motor
  Museum; Polegate Windmill and
  Miller Museum
Pulborough: Bignor Roman Villa
Rye: Rye Heritage Centre; Ypres Tower
  Museum
Seaford: Seaford Museum of Local
  History
Shoreham-by-Sea: Henfield Museum;
  Marlipins Museum

Steyning: Steyning Museum Trust
Uckfield: Bridge Cottage; Heaven Farm
  Country Tours and Museum;
  Lavender Line Steam Museum
Winchelsea: Winchelsea Museum
Worthing: Worthing Museum and Art
  Gallery

Natural History

The region is scattered with nature reserves that often have trails, hides and information centres, some also have guides. There are also several animal sanctuaries, unusual animal collections in natural surroundings, and conservation centres that are fascinating to visit.

KENT

Bromley: Crystal Palace Tree Trail; High Elms Nature Reserve; Kelsey Park; Seadbury Park Nature Reserve
Dartford: Joydens Wood
Faversham: Perry Wood; South Swale Nature Reserve
Gillingham: Berengrave Nature Reserve
Minster-in-Sheppey: Leysdown Coastal Park
Ramsgate: Pegwell Bay
Sevenoaks: Bough Beech Nature Reserve; Sevenoaks Wildfowl Reserve
Sheerness: Elmley Marshes
Sittingbourne: Queendown Warren Nature Reserve

SURREY

Dorking: Box Hill; The Sheepleas
Godalming: Witley Common
Reigate: Laporte Earth's Park Woods Nature Trail; New Pond Farm and Felland Wood
Woking: Surrey Wildlife Trust

SUSSEX

Pulborough: The Old Rectory Adult Education College
Rye: Rye Harbour Nature Reserve
Seaford: The Living World
Steyning: Woods Mill Countryside Centre

Ornamental Parks

Ornamental parks provide colourful, fragrant recreational areas where you can take a stroll or take a seat and watch the world go by. They vary in size, elaboration and theme from town to town but always provide pleasure to those passing through them and to the wildlife who make them their habitat.

KENT

Bromley: Church House Gardens; Priory Gardens

SURREY

Guildford: Stoke Park

SUSSEX

Arundel: Swanbourne Lake and Park
Bognor Regis: Hotham Park

Crawley: Memorial Gardens
Eastbourne: Carpet Gardens; Devonshire Park; Gildredge Park; Hampden Park; Helen Gardens; Princes Park
Hastings: Alexandra Park; White Rock Gardens
St Leonards: St Leonards Gardens
Worthing: Beach House Park; Denton Gardens; Field Place; Marine Gardens; Steyne Gardens

Piers & Promenades

Piers and promenades are a feature of the seaside towns that grew into popular resorts during the Victorian and Edwardian eras. The piers offer traditional seaside amusements, miniature railways, fun fairs for the children and some have theatres that open for the summer season. The promenades along the seafronts often have delightful flower displays. They offer perfect vantage points to sit and watch the world go by.

KENT

Deal: Deal Pier
Folkestone: Leas Promenade

SUSSEX

Brighton: Brighton Pier
Eastbourne: Eastbourne Pier; Eastbourne Promenade
Hastings: Hastings Pier
Worthing: Worthing Pier; Seafront Promenade

Railways

Very few of us fail to respond to the delights of steam railways, entwined as they are with tales of our childhood. The heartening hoots they make as they puff by bring storybook pictures alive – try some of their special rides!

KENT

Dartford: North Downs Steam Railway
Dymchurch: Romney, Hythe and Dymchurch Railway
Hythe: Romney, Hythe and Dymchurch Railway
Maidstone: Mote Park
New Romney: Romney, Hythe and Dymchurch Railway

Sittingbourne: Sittingbourne and Kemsley Light Railway
Tenterden: Kent and East Sussex Railway

SURREY

Chertsey: Great Cockcrow Railway

Romney, Hythe and Dymchurch Railway

Bluebell Railway

SUSSEX

Brighton: Volks Electric Railway
Hastings: East and West Hill Cliff Railways
Lewes: Bentley Wildfowl and Motor Museum

Rye: Kent and East Sussex Steam Railway
Uckfield: Bluebell Railway; Lavender Line Steam Museum

Kent and East Sussex Steam Railway

Theatres

The south-east has a wide selection of theatres. The coastal resorts have a range of summer season shows and the major towns of the region produce many innovative and acclaimed productions as well as the more familiar and much loved classics.

KENT

Bromley: The Bromley Little Theatre; Churchill Theatre
Canterbury: Gulbenkian Theatre; Marlowe Theatre
Chatham: Medway Arts Centre
Dartford: Orchard Theatre
Faversham: Ardent Theatre
Folkestone: Leas Cliff Hall; Metropole Arts Centre
Gravesend: Woodville Halls
Leeds: Leeds Castle
Maidstone: Hazlitt Theatre
Margate: Theatre Royal; Tom Thumb Theatre; Winter Gardens Theatre
Royal Tunbridge Wells: Trinity Theatre and Arts Centre
Sevenoaks: Stag Theatre
Whitstable: The Playhouse

SURREY

Camberley: Civic Hall
Dorking: Dorking Halls
Epsom: Adrian Mann Theatre; Bourne Hall; Epsom Playhouse
Farnham: The Redgrave Theatre

Guildford: Yvonne Arnaud Theatre; Civic Hall
Leatherhead: Thorndike Theatre
Reigate: Harlequin Theatre
Woking: QEII Theatre and Cinema

SUSSEX

Arundel: The Priory Playhouse
Bexhill-on-Sea: De La Warr Pavilion
Bognor Regis: Bognor Regis Centre
Brighton: Theatre Royal; The Brighton Centre; The Dome Complex; Gardner Theatre
Burwash: Bateman's
Chichester: Festival Theatre
Crawley: The Hawth
Eastbourne: Congress Theatre; Devonshire Park Theatre; Royal Hippodrome; Winter Garden Theatre
Hastings: Stables Theatre; White Rock Theatre
Littlehampton: The Windmill
St Leonards: Marina Pavilion
Worthing: Pavilion Theatre; Connaught Theatre; Assembly Hall

Theme Parks

There is everything you can ride or climb on – scary rides or animated reality and futuristic themes at the Chessington World of Aventures. Unforgettable days out for children and many adults too!

KENT

Margate: Bembom Brothers White Knuckle Theme Park

SURREY

Epsom: Chessington World of Adventures

SUSSEX

Eastbourne: Fort Fun; Treasure Island
Hastings: Smugglers Adventure

Chessington World of Adventures

Wildlife Parks

Many people have directed their love of animals and wildlife into the collection and breeding of often rare and exotic species. This has over recent years led to the opening of their collections to the public. Set in acres of ground the wildlife are kept in pleasant surroundings and the parks often have amenities for children such as pets corners, adventure playgrounds and picnic sites.

KENT

Canterbury: Blean Bird Park; Wingham Bird Park
Dover: The Butterfly Centre
Folkestone: The Butterfly Centre
Herne Bay: Brambles English Wildlife and Rare Breeds

SURREY

Farnham: Birdworld

SUSSEX

Alfriston: Drusillas Park
Chichester: Earnley Butterflies and Gardens
Eastbourne: The Butterfly Centre
East Grinstead: Spring Hill Wildfowl Park
Lewes: Bentley Wildfowl and Motor Museum; Raysted Centre for Animal Welfare

Special Interests

Zoos

Tigers, lions, leopards, elephants, monkeys, bears, even snakes and insects are a source of continual fascination to all ages, so what better way to spend a day than wandering around the zoo reminding oneself of the other inhabitants of our world and enjoying their interesting and often funny habits.

KENT

Bromley: Crystal Palace Park
Canterbury: Howletts Zoo
Hythe: Port Lympne Zoo Park

SUSSEX

Crawley: Gatwick Zoo
Rye: The Children's Farm

SURREY

Epsom: Chessington Zoo

Water Sports

Boat Hire

Explore the countryside from the water, discover remote backwaters, enjoy the wildlife of the river-banks and marshes, cruise gently along or stop at some of the riverside pubs. Boats can be hired from many centres around the region and, as with many of the facilities included in this guide, it is wise to telephone for information about the vessels available and the terms and conditions of hire. Everyone interested can try 'messing about on the river' in a wide selection of craft ranging from small motor cabin cruisers to barges, all-weather day launches to rowing boats.

SURREY

Godalming: Farncombe Boat House
Guildford: Guildford Boathouse

SUSSEX

Arundel: Bullers Boatyard; Swanbourne Lake
Eastbourne: Bluebird Speedboats

Boating on the River Thames

Boat Trips

For those who have no wish to captain their own vessel there are several organised boat trips to enjoy. There is a craft to suit everyone, steamer, pleasure barge or motor launch – whatever appeals. All sorts of refreshments and entertainments are available on the larger boats for individuals or groups.

KENT

Chatham: Kingswear Castle Excursions Ltd
Lamberhurst: Bewl Water
Maidstone: *Kentish Lady II*
Rochester: Invicta Line Cruises
Tonbridge: Caxton Tonbridge Waterways

SURREY

Chertsey: French Brothers
Guildford: Guildford Boathouse

SUSSEX

Arundel: River Arun Cruises
Chichester: Chichester Harbour Water Tours
Eastbourne: Allchorn Brothers; Bluebird Speedboats
Littlehampton: River Arun Cruises

Canoeing

Canoeing appeals to a wide cross-section of people as you can choose between expeditions on calm waters or the challenge of pitting yourself against the wilder waters found in rivers with rapids and in the sea. Types of water are classified by the British Canoe Union and they range from placid water, white water Grades I to III and river, estuary, harbour through to sea and surf. To begin canoeing it is wise to seek expert guidance to learn the simple techniques and safety measures. There are many approved centres and the Canoe Union will supply a list on request from the address given below. Interestingly very few people learn to 'canoe' as canoes are open boats propelled by a single-bladed paddle – most people learn to 'kayak' in kayaks where they sit right inside propelled by a doubled-bladed paddle.

British Canoe Union
Adbolton Lane
West Bridgford
Nottingham
☎ 0602 821100

KENT

Bromley: Beckenham Leisure Centre
Canterbury: Riverside Outdoor
    Education
Margate: Thanet Canoe Club
Rochester: Arethusa Venture Centre

SURREY

Weybridge: Addlestone Canoe Club

SUSSEX

Eastbourne: Cuckmere Valley Canoe
    Club

Diving

Treasure troves beneath the sea, whether old galleons or brilliant and bizarre underwater sea creatures, attract many people to take up diving. Modern equipment is extremely light compared with the diving suits once worn so anyone who can swim and who is reasonably fit can try out an introductory diving course. The British Sub-Aqua Club (BSAC), the governing body of the sport, are known for the high standards they set and by following a course at a diving school or by joining one of the BSAC clubs it should be possible to attain their Novice Diver standard over three to six months. Continuing on to obtain the Sport Diver status will equip a diver to dive anywhere in the world in the company of other qualified divers. Underwater photography in tropical waters or exploring wrecks can begin with trying out an aqualung in a swimming pool. For more information contact the BSAC at the address given.

British Sub-Aqua Club (BSAC)
Talfords Quay, Ellesmere Port,
Cheshire
☎ 051 357 1951

KENT

Gillingham: South East Diving Centre

SURREY

Woking: Surrey Aquanauts

SUSSEX

Littlehampton: Arun Divers

Jet-Skiing

Jet-skiing is another exciting watersport for the adventure seeking water lover. There is only one place that offers opportunities to pursue this sport in this region at present but many of the numerous watersports centres will no doubt be including it in the near future.

KENT

Margate: Water Sports International

Swimming

Swimming remains one of the most enjoyable and therapeutic of the watersports. The leisure centres throughout the region often have very exotic pool surrounds and include aquaslides, whirlpools and inflatables to provide extra fun in the water.

KENT

Bromley: Beckenham Leisure Centre; Darrick Wood Pool; National Recreation Centre; Walnut Sports Centre; West Wickham Pools
Dartford: FantaSeas
Deal: Tides Leisure Pool
Faversham: Faversham Pool
Folkestone: Folkestone Sports Centre
Gillingham: Splashes Swimming Pool
Gravesend: Cascades Leisure Centre
Margate: Hartsdown Park Sports and Leisure Centre
Northfleet: Cygnet Leisure Centre; Northfleet Pool
Rochester: Hundred of Hoo Pool; Strood Sports Centre
Royal Tunbridge Wells: Sports and 'Y' Centre
Sevenoaks: Sevenoaks Swimming Centre
Sittingbourne: The Swallows

SURREY

Camberley: Arena Leisure Centre
Dorking: Dorking Swimming Centre
Epsom: Rainbow Centre
Farnham: Farnham Sports Centre
Godalming: Godalming Leisure Centre
Guildford: Guildford Lido
Haslemere: Haslemere Swimming Pool and Squash Courts
Horley: Horley Swimming Pool
Reigate: Donyngs Recreation Centre
Walton-on-Thames: Walton Swimming Pool
Woking: Pool in the Park

SUSSEX

Arundel: Arundel Swimming Pool
Bexhill-on-Sea: Bexhill Leisure Pool
Brighton: Prince Regent Swimming Complex
Chichester: Westgate Centre
Crowborough: Goldsmiths Swimming Pool
Eastbourne: Motcombe Swimming Pool; Sovereign Centre
East Grinstead: Kings Centre
Haywards Heath: Dolphin Leisure Centre
Horsham: Park Swimming Centre
Hove: King Alfred Leisure Centre
Lewes: The Pells
Littlehampton: Swimming & Sports Centre
Newhaven: Seahaven Pool
Seaford: Seaford Head Pool
Worthing: Aquarena

Water-Skiing

Water-skiing is an exhilarating sport and can be safely pursued at one of the clubs affiliated to the British Water Ski Federation. Basic equipment is usually provided and there are opportunities to develop the skill and confidence necessary to progress to jumps and competitions. For information and a list of clubs with details of their facilities contact the British Water Ski Federation at the address given below.

British Water Ski Federation
390 City Road
London
☎ 071 833 2855/6

KENT

Lydd: Lydd Water Ski Club
Margate: Fornesse Water-Ski Club
Ramsgate: Seawide Leisure
Whitstable: Seasalter Water Ski

SUSSEX

Bexhill-on-Sea: Bexhill Beach
Rye: Rye Water-Ski Club

Windsurfing

Windsurfing, or boardsailing as it is also known, has become very popular and the colourful sails and characteristic silhouettes of the windsurfers are a familiar sight on many lakes and off many beaches. The relative ease with which windsurfers can be transported makes it a fairly flexible sport to pursue. To learn to windsurf it is advisable to approach a school approved by the Royal Yachting Association; most will supply boards, sails and wetsuits. You will be taken through the techniques involved on dry land before taking to the water and then over a couple of days you will learn how to sail a course, how to rig a board and how to observe the rules of safety for yourself and other water users. A beginners course does not involve a huge outlay and it might introduce you to an exciting new sport. Contact the Windsurfing Information Centre at the Royal Yachting Association for more details.

The Windsurfing Information Centre
Royal Yachting Association
Romsey Road
Eastleigh
Hampshire
☎ 0703 629962

KENT

Lydd: Romney Marsh Windsurfing Centre
Sheerness: Woods Mill Countryside Centre

SUSSEX

Bexhill-on-Sea: Rother Coastline
Brighton: Hove Lagoon Watersports Centre Ltd; Sun Sports
Chichester: Chichester Sailing Centre
Crawley: Tilgate Park
Littlehampton: Angmering Windsurfing

SURREY

Caterham: Mercers Park Windsurfing

Yacht Charter

Yacht charter provides the opportunity to enjoy sailing holidays on a variety of boats that you do not have to maintain all the year round, or indeed invest in, in the first place. Skippered charter is relatively risk-free as the skipper usually knows his boat. For self-sail charter it is advisable to charter the boat from a company who will give you an introduction into handling the craft. For advice and information to help you select your charter contact the Yacht Charter Association at the address below.

Yacht Charter Association
60 Silverdale
New Milton
Hants
☎ 0425 619004

SUSSEX

Bexhill-on-Sea: Brighton Marina Sea School
Brighton: Brighton Marina

Water Sports

Yachting

Yachting, yacht cruising and dinghy sailing are enjoyable to people of all ages and the south-east provides some excellent sailing opportunities. There are many yacht clubs, some of which will offer cruising courses for those interested in learning to sail or for those who wish to broaden their experience. For details and information about yachting and courses contact the Royal Yachting Association at the address below.

Royal Yachting Association
Romsey Road
Eastleigh
Hampshire
☎ 0703 629962

KENT

Broadstairs: Broadstairs Sailing Club
Chatham: Medway Sea School
Deal: Dover Sea School
Dover: Kent Sailing School
Gillingham: Gillingham Marina
Gravesend: Gravesend Sailing Club;
    North Kent Yachting Association
Herne Bay: Herne Bay Yacht Club;
    Herne Bay Sailing Club Ltd
Lamberhurst: Bewl Water
Tonbridge: Chipstead Sailing Club
Whitstable: Whitstable Yacht Club

SURREY

Farnham: Simanda Yachting Services
Woking: Oystercat Cruises

SUSSEX

Bexhill-on-Sea: Bexhill Sailing Club
Bognor Regis: Bognor Regis Yacht Club;
    Felpham Yacht Club
Brighton: Brighton Marina Sea School;
    Brighton Marina Village; Brighton
    Marina Yacht Club; Brighton Sailing
    Club; Sussex Motor Yacht Club
Chichester: Chichester Sailing Centre;
    The Solent Coastal and Offshore
    Sailing School
Hove: Marabu Syndicate
Littlehampton: Littlehampton Marina;
    Offshore Sailing School
St Leonards: Hastings & St Leonards
    Sailing Club

Winter Sports

Skiing

The south-east is not noted for its snow-capped mountain slopes but lovers of skiing can still enjoy their sport on any of the dry slopes in the region. For more information about skiing in Britain contact the British Ski Federation at the address below.

British Ski Federation
58 Main Street
East Calder
West Lothian
    0506 884343

KENT

Chatham: The Alpine Ski Centre
Folkestone: Folkestone Sports Centre

SURREY

Esher: Sandown Ski School
Guildford: Bishop Reindorp Ski School

SUSSEX

Newhaven: Borowski Ski Centre

Places

Discover the south-eastern counties of Kent, Surrey and Sussex. Despite being so close to London this area retains many fascinating and relatively unexplored corners. There are picturesque villages, elegant stately homes, historic centres, cathedral cities with their many treasures, lonely stretches of shoreline, and splendid Victorian and Edwardian seaside towns. There is much to do and plenty to see.

Select the city, town or village you wish to visit (they are arranged alphabetically) and you will find a description, local information, and a detailed list of leisure activities with the telephone number, address or access information and any other interesting details. If you want to know more about a particular activity look it up in the activities section where you will find general information about it, the name and address of the governing body plus a list of all the places in the region where you can enjoy the activity. You might find a familiar place has unexpected opportunities to enjoy a favourite pursuit or an unfamiliar place is much more exciting than you expected!

Guide to symbols

- *i*   tourist information centre
    (✳ Not open all year)
- ⌐₁₈   18-hole golf course
- ⌐₉   9-hole golf course
- P   car parking
- ✝   abbey, cathedral, church of interest
- 🏛   historic building, historic house, historic property
- 🏛   museum, art gallery
- ⇌   BR station
- Ⓧ   leisure centre, sports centre, swimming pool
- →   one-way streets

The Pantiles, Royal Tunbridge Wells

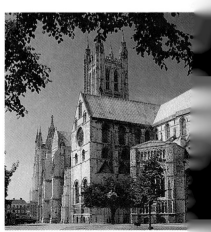

Canterbury Cathedral

Alfriston can be found in the heart of the Cuckmere Valley in East Sussex. The changing aspects of Alfriston since it was a Saxon settlement are displayed at the heritage centre. The village has many notable old houses including the 14th century Clergy House which was the first building to be purchased by the National Trust. One of England's smallest churches can be found just across the river at Lullington. The River Cuckmere was once a haunt for smugglers when it was navigable up to Alfriston; now, a rich habitat for wildlife, it is ideal for walking and fishing.

i Seaford
Station Approach
☎ 0323 897426

Early closing Wednesday
Population 800

Aerial Sports

GLIDING

East Sussex Gliding Club
5 miles east of Ringmer on the B2192
Winch flights.
☎ 0825 84 347

Outdoor Leisure

FISHING

Coarse Fishing
Fishing on both banks of the Cuckmere. For information and permits contact the National Rivers Authority, Coast Road, Pevensey Bay, East Sussex.
☎ 0323 762691

Seaford and Newhaven Angling Club
Contact Mr G R Martin, 4 South Road, Newhaven
☎ 0273 516849

HORSE RIDING

Vinton Street Farm Stables
Vinton Street
General instruction, hacking and livery.
☎ 0323 870089

WALKING AND RAMBLING

South Downs Way
96-mile long distance route, the only one open to horseriders and cyclists too. Delightful views of the sea and the downs.

Special Interests

ARTS AND CRAFTS

Drusillas Park
Craftsmen at work; shops.
☎ 0323 870234

FOOD AND DRINK

The English Wine Centre
Drusillas Corner
Tours of vineyard, cellars and wine museum. English Wine Festival in September.
☎ 0323 870164

HERITAGE

Long Man of Wilmington
East of Alfriston at Wilmington
A 200-foot Long Man carved in the chalk hillside.

HISTORIC BUILDINGS

Lullington Church
1 mile east of Alfriston
Reputedly the smallest church in England; good views.

St Andrews Church
The Tye
14th century church known as the 'Cathedral of the Downs'.

The Old Clergy House
The Tye
14th century half-timbered building beside Alfriston Church. The first building acquired by the National Trust (1896). Garden and shop.
☎ 0323 870001

MUSEUMS

Alfriston Heritage Centre and Blacksmiths Museum
The Old Forge, Sloe Lane
18th century buildings with farriers and blacksmiths museum; local history.
☎ 0323 870303

61

Wilmington Priory
The Street, Wilmington
Remains of a 13th century Benedictine
priory housing agricultural exhibits.
The 'Long Man of Wilmington' can be
seen from the priory.
☎ 0323 870537

WILDLIFE PARKS

Drusillas Park
Wide and varied range of animals, birds
and butterflies in natural settings;
miniature railway; farmyard; award
winning gardens.
☎ 0323 870234

Arundel is situated in the beautiful Arun Valley where the River Arun cuts through
the South Downs. The castle, built by the Normans to protect the valley from sea
raiders, dominates the skyline above the town. It is the ancestral home of the Duke of
Norfolk, whose flag can be seen flying above its fairy-tale like turrets. The town, once a
thriving port, is mostly Victorian with some flint-walled cottages and several 18th
century buildings.

Arundel is an ideal centre for touring the surrounding countryside – there are
cruises up the river, there are cycling, riding and walking routes across the Downs
and there is good sport for the racing enthusiast at the national hunt racecourse at
Fontwell Park.

i 61 High Street
☎ 0903 882268

Early closing Wednesday
Population 2788

Outdoor Leisure

BIRDWATCHING

Wildfowl and Wetlands Centre
Mill Road
1000 ducks, geese and swans set amidst
the Sussex Downs beneath Arundel
Castle. Wildfowl Trust.
☎ 0903 883355

CYCLING

Cycling Round West Sussex
The Tourist Information Centre
publishes a useful leaflet entitled
Cycling Round West Sussex.

FISHING

Coarse Fishing
Fishing from Arundel Bridge, to the
south of Stoke Bridge and Bupham
backwater, Rivers Arun and Rother. For
information and permits, contact the
National Rivers Authority at Pevensey
Bay.
☎ 0323 762691

Binstead Pond
Day tickets available from Mrs Jeffry,
3C Fitzalam Road.

Game Fishing

Sussex County Angling Association
Day tickets available from G & A
Shepherd, 10 High Street.

Chalk Springs Trout Fishery
Day tickets available from Mr J Glover,
Chalk Springs, Park Bottom.
☎ 0903 883742

HORSE RACING

Fontwell Park Racecourse
Eastergate
A 1-mile, figure of eight course hosting
15 national hunt race days each year.
☎ 0243 543335

HORSE RIDING

Arundel Riding Centre
Park Place
Lessons; dressage; show jumping
and eventing.
☎ 0903 882061

WALKING AND RAMBLING

The Tourist Information Centre
supplies leaflets of walks in the area.
Information can also be obtained from
the County Planning Department.
☎ 0243 777420

Special Interests

ANTIQUES

Arundel Bridge Antiques
☎ 0903 884164

ARTS AND CRAFTS

The Arundel Fine Glass & Engraving Studio
Tarrant Square, Tarrant Street
☎ 0903 883597

ART GALLERIES

River Gallery
25 High Street
Fine art dealers; regular exhibitions in a historic building.
☎ 0903 882177

Arundel Castle
Private art and furniture collection from the 16th century.
☎ 0903 883136

FESTIVALS AND FAIRS

May
Corpus Christi Flowers and Floral Festival at Arundel Cathedral.

August/September
Arundel Festival – open air festival under the battlements of Arundel Castle. Programme includes concerts, Shakespeare and jazz.
☎ 0903 883690

FOOD AND DRINK

Arundel Vineyards
Church Lane, Lyminster
A small vineyard and winery housed in a barn.
0903 883393

GARDENS

Denmans Gardens
Fontwell
Various different garden styles including walled, gravel, herb and wild gardens. Gift and tea shop.
0243 542808

GUIDED TOURS

Mary Godby
Stable House, Amberley
Specialising in West Sussex town walks, coach tours and visits.
0798 831614

HISTORIC BUILDINGS

Arundel Castle
Restored Norman castle with an 11th century keep and 13th century barbican. The ancestral home of the Duke of Norfolk, it houses a collection of art and furniture from the 16th century.
☎ 0903 883136

Arundel Cathedral
Famous for the 97 foot long 'carpet of flowers' celebrating the Feastday and created by the ladies of the cathedral parish – a tradition since 1877.
☎ 0903 882297

Arundel Castle

MUSEUMS

Amberley Chalk Pits Museum
Houghton Bridge, Amberley
Industrial history, working trades displays.
☎ 0798 831370

Arundel Museum and Heritage Centre
61 High Street
Nine galleries depicting Arundel from prehistory to the present day.
☎ 0903 882274

Arundel Toy and Military Museum
23 High Street
An extensive private collection of old toys.
☎ 0903 883101/882908

ORNAMENTAL PARKS

Swanbourne Lake and Park
Relaxing site for picnics with good views of the Downs. Cars, motor bikes, bicycles and dogs not permitted in the park.

THEATRES

The Priory Playhouse
London Road
Shows by the Arundel Players throughout the year.
☎ 0903 883345

Water Sports

BOAT HIRE

Bullers Boatyard
Mill Road
☎ 0903 882609

Swanbourne Lake
Arundel Park
Rowing boats available for hire
between May and September.

BOAT TRIPS

River Arun Cruises
2 Railway Cottages, The Causeway
Historical, wildlife or musical
programmes available for cruises up the
Arun Valley.
☎ 0903 883920

SWIMMING

Arundel Swimming Pool
Heated open-air swimming pool. Open
May – September.
☎ 0903 882404

Ashford is situated on a tributary of the East Stour river in Kent. The town, now a
regional shopping centre, expanded rapidly with the development of the railway. It
has retained several mediaeval houses, a reminder of the small village it once was. It
is surrounded by many attractive and interesting villages.

i Lower High Street
☎ 0233 629165

Market days Tuesday, Saturday
Early closing Wednesday
Population 46,962

Aerial Sports

GLIDING

Kent Gliding Club
Squids Gate, Challock
☎ 0233 74 307/274

PARACHUTING

Headcorn Parachute Centre
The Airfield, Headcorn
Parachuting: from beginners to
skydiving.
☎ 0622 890862

Slipstream Adventures
The Airfield, Headcorn
☎ 0622 890641

Multi-Activity Holidays

MULTI-ACTIVITY CENTRES

Hazel Tree Farm
Hassell Street, Hastingleigh
Weekend courses; word processing,
flower arranging and painting.
☎ 0233 75324

Shopping Centre, Ashford

SPECIAL INTEREST CENTRES

Rooting St Farm Riding Centre
Little Chart
Courses and tuition for adults and
children.
☎ 0233 84434

Outdoor Leisure

FISHING

Coarse Fishing
Fishing on the River Stour, the Royal
Military Canal, Iden Lock to Appledore
and Appledore to West Hythe (south
bank only). For information and
permits contact the National Rivers
Authority.

Chequer Tree Farm
Bethersden
☎ 0233 82383

Singleton Lake
For permits and day tickets apply to
the Ashford Council.
☎ 0233 637311

GOLF

Ashford (Kent) Golf Club 🏌
Sandyhurst Lane
Handicap certificate required.
☎ 0223 620180

HORSE RIDING

Blue Barn Equestrian Centre
Blue Barn Farm, Great Chart
Residential holiday instruction in
riding and jumping, hacking, schooling
and showing.
☎ 0233 622933/621183

Oathill Farm Riding Centre
Pound Lane, Molash
Riding holidays, hacking, general
instruction.
☎ 0233 74 573

Special Interests

ART GALLERIES

Evegate Farm Art Gallery
Station Road, Smeeth
Original paintings and varied crafts.
☎ 0303 813687

FOOD AND DRINK

Headcorn Flowers and Vineyard
Grigg Lane, Headcorn
Tours of heated flowerhouses
concluding with wine tasting.
☎ 0622 890250

GARDENS

Godinton House Gardens
Godinton Park
18th century gardens with topiary.
☎ 0233 620773

HISTORIC HOUSES

Godinton House
Godinton Park
Jacobean house with fine carving and
panelling, porcelain and picture
collections.
☎ 0233 620773

MUSEUMS

Local History Museum
Central Library, Church Road
Trade, rural, domestic and wartime
exhibits.
☎ 0233 620649

Wye College Agricultural Museum
14th century tithe barn and 19th
century oast house with a collection of
farm tools and implements.
☎ 0233 812401

Banstead lies within Surrey's Green Belt and is surrounded by the North Downs. The 2000 acres of commons and open downlands includes Walton Heath with its famous golf courses – this is an ideal centre for golfing and riding. The town is mainly residential with a busy shopping centre. It is linked to the centre of London, only 15 miles away, by regular rail services. Banstead's 12th century church has a shingled tower and a west window designed by the renowned pre-Raphaelites, William Morris and Rossetti. In the surrounding area are Chipstead and Walton-on-the-Hill; both are predominantly Victorian villages.

i Katherine Street
Croydon
☎ 081 760 5630

Early closing Wednesday
Population 46,163

Indoor Sports

LEISURE CENTRES

Banstead Sports Centre
Merland Rise, Tadworth
Swimming pool, ball games, racquet sports facilities, sauna and sunbeds available.
☎ 0737 361933

Outdoor Leisure

GOLF

Banstead Downs Golf Club ⚐
Burdon Lane, Belmont, Sutton
Downland course with narrow fairways and hawthorns. Handicap required.
☎ 081 642 2284/6884

Chipstead Golf Club Ltd ⚐
How Lane, Chipstead
Visitors welcome on weekdays and at weekends accompanied by a member.
☎ 0737 555781

Coulsden Court Golf Club ⚐
Coulsden Road, Coulsden
Visitors welcome.
☎ 081 660 6083

Kingswood Golf and Country Club ⚐
Sandy Lane, Tadworth
Visitors welcome except before 11.30 am on weekend.
☎ 0737 832188

The Oaks Sports Centre ⚐ ⚐
Woodmansterne Road, Carshalton Beeches
☎ 081 643 8363

Walton Heath Golf Club ⚐
Deans Lane, Tadworth
Visitors welcome by prior arrangement.
☎ 0737 812380

HORSE RIDING

The Clock Tower Riding Centre
Brighton Road, Kingswood, Tadworth
Hacking in superb riding country with no roadwork necessary.
☎ 0737 832874

Huntersfield Farm Riding Centre
Fairlawn Road (off Croydon Lane)
☎ 081 643 1333

Orchard Cottage Riding Stables
Babylon Lane, Lower Kingswood
General purpose hacks on the South Downs and common land. Riding for beginners.
☎ 0737 241311

Wildwoods Riding Centre
Ebbisham Lane, Walton on the Hill, Tadworth
Hacking on heath and forest areas, general instruction and riding club.
☎ 0737 812146

TENNIS

Transworld Tennis
Tuckaway, Warren Drive, Kingswood
Tennis holidays in the UK and overseas.
☎ 0737 832009

Special Interests

ANTIQUES

Carshalton Antique Gallery
5 High Street, Carshalton
☎ 081 647 5664

COUNTRY PARKS

The Banstead Commons
Banstead Downs, 430 acres; Banstead Heath, 760 acres; Burgh Heath, 87 acres and Park Downs, 74 acres.
Opportunities for walking, horse riding, games and picnicking. Telephone the Clerk of the Conservators,
Mr R MacKay, for further details.
☎ 0737 842251

Nork Park
West of Banstead on the A240
100 acres of woodland and open space which is partly in agricultural use.

HISTORIC BUILDINGS

All Saints Church
12th century two-bay nave, octagonal Caen stone font and a west window designed by Rosetti and Morris.

SUSSEX

Battle

SUSSEX

Battle is a charming mediaeval town dominated by its magnificent abbey. The town and the abbey were built on the site of the famous Battle of Hastings fought in 1066 between William the Conqueror and Harold, the Saxon King of England.

i 88 High Street
☎ 0424 63721

Market Day Friday
Population 5300

Outdoor Leisure

FISHING

Coarse Fishing
Farthings Lake
Day tickets from 23 Manley Rise.

Wyland Farm and Lakes
Powdermill Lane, Catsfield
Six lakes set in 150 acres; chalets for hire.
☎ 0424 892963

WALKING AND RAMBLING

Walks around Battle
The Tourist Information Office will provide details of Battle Ramblers Association walks 1–7.

Special Interests

FACTORY TOURS

Carr Taylor Vineyards
Tours of the winery.
☎ 0424 752501

FESTIVALS AND FAIRS

March/April
Marbles Match on Good Friday at the Abbey Green.

May
Ten day Music and Drama Festival.

November
Battle Bonfire and Torchlight Procession.

FOOD AND DRINK

Carr Taylor Vineyards
6 miles south-east between the A21 and the A28 at Westfield
Modern winery with a lovely barn for wine tasting.
☎ 0424 752501

HISTORIC BUILDINGS

Battle Abbey
High Street
Ruins of a Benedictine abbey built by William the Conquerer to commemorate the Battle of Hastings, fought on this site in 1066.
☎ 0424 63792

St Mary's
A Norman church built by monks in 1150.

MUSEUMS

Battle Museum
Langton House
Relics and exhibits of Normans, Saxons and the Battle of 1066.

Buckley's Museum of Shops
90 High Street
Arcade of preserved Edwardian shops with over 30,000 exhibits.
☎ 0424 64269

Bexhill-on-Sea is a quiet, relaxing coastal resort which developed along the shingle beach during the late Victorian and Edwardian eras. The seafront is dominated by the magnificent De La Warr Pavilion, an international-style entertainment centre built in the 1930s by two German architects, Erich Mendelssohn and Sergey Chermayeff. The award-winning beach offers a wide range of activities such as windsurfing and sailing and the town's lovely gardens, inviting coastal walks and range of leisure facilities have made it a very popular coastal resort.

i De La Warr Pavilion
☎ 0424 212023

Market day Tuesday
Early closing Wednesday
Population 35,529

Indoor Sports

LEISURE CENTRES

Bexhill Leisure Centre
Down Road
A 'dry-centre' with facilities for racquet sports, fitness training, a sauna and solarium and children's holiday clubs. Restaurant and bar facilities are also available and membership is not required.
☎ 0424 731171

TEN PIN BOWLING

GX Superbowl
Hastings Road
24 lanes.
☎ 0424 730014

Outdoor Leisure

FISHING

Coarse Fishing

Hastings and Bexhill Angling Club
☎ 0424 852678

Game Fishing

Hastings Fly Fishers Club Ltd
Mr D E Tack, 23 Wealdon Way, Little Common
☎ 042 43 3957

Sea Fishing
Contact the Tourist Information Centre for details.
☎ 0424 212023

GOLF

Cooden Beach Golf Club ⛳₁₈
Cooden Beach
Seaside course. Visitors welcome, preferably by prior arrangement.
☎ 042 43 2040/3938

Highwoods Golf Club ⛳₁₈
Ellerslie Lane
Handicap certificate required; visitors must be accompanied by a member at weekends.
☎ 0424 212625/212770

TENNIS

Bexhill Tennis Club
Courts available to visitors, contact the Secretary, Mrs J Wood.
☎ 042 43 5381

Special Interests

COUNTRY PARKS

Broad Oak Country Park
2 miles from town centre, follow signs from the A259
Picnic among the trees or try the small fitness trail.
☎ 0424 220620

FESTIVALS AND FAIRS

May
Horse Show

September
Music Festival

MUSEUMS

Bexhill Museum
Egerton Road
Local and natural history, archaeology and geology exhibits.
☎ 0424 211769

Bexhill Museum of Costume and Social History
Period costumes from 1740–1960.
☎ 0424 215361

THEATRES

De La Warr Pavilion
Shows throughout the year.
☎ 0424 210045

Water Sports

SWIMMING

Bexhill Leisure Pool
Ravenside Retail and Leisure Park
Water-slide, wave-machine pool,
gym, sauna and solarium.
☎ 0424 731508

WATER-SKIING

Boats may be launched from Bexhill
Beach.

WINDSURFING

Rother coastline towards Eastbourne is
very popular for windsurfing.

YACHTING

Bexhill Sailing Club
De La Warr Parade
Affiliated with the RYA.
☎ 0424 212906

YACHT CHARTER

Brighton Marina Sea School
97 De La Warr Road
Yachts available for charter; tuition also
available for certificates – book in
advance for spring/summer months.
☎ 0273 600044

KENT / **Biggin Hill** \ KENT

Biggin Hill is famous for its Battle of Britain airfield. It has a chapel commemorating
pilots stationed there who died in the war. Not surprisingly the airfield is a centre for
flying schools and clubs. It also houses one of the first hang gliding schools to be
established in Britain. Situated on a plateau of the North Downs it is a good riding
and walking centre and it has several golf courses in its vicinity.

Aerial Sports

FLYING

Air Touring Club
Biggin Hill Airport
☎ 0959 73133

Biggin Hill School of Flying
Biggin Hill Airport
☎ 0959 73583

Kingair School of Flying
Biggin Hill Airport
☎ 0959 75088

Surrey and Kent Flying Club
Biggin Hill Airport
☎ 0959 72255

HANG GLIDING

Skyriders
15 St Mary's Green
One of the first schools established in
Britain. Offers two day basic courses,
Elementary Pilot Certificate and Club
Pilot Certificate Courses.
☎ 0959 73996

Outdoor Leisure

GOLF

Addington Court Golf Courses ⛳₁₈
Featherbed Lane, Addington
Two 18 hole courses, visitors welcome.
☎ 081 657 0281

Cherry Lodge Golf Club 🏌18
Jail Lane
Parkland course with good views; sauna available.
☎ 0959 72250

High Elms Golf Club 🏌18
High Elms Road, Downe
Parkland course, unrestricted for visitors.
☎ 0689 858175
☎ 081 300 2734

HORSE RIDING

Chavic Park Farm
Jail Lane
General instruction in riding, jumping and livery.
☎ 0959 72090

Greenacres Riding School Ltd
Greenaces, Ashmore Lane, Leaves Green, Keston
Residential instructional holidays in riding, jumping and livery. Four annual horse shows.
☎ 0959 72008

SUSSEX / **Bodiam** SUSSEX

Bodiam is situated inland from the East Sussex coastline in an area where there are no large towns and the settlements are mainly villages. Bodiam is famous for its beautiful fairy-tale castle built in 1388 to defend the River Rother from French invaders who never came.

Outdoor Leisure

FISHING

Coarse Fishing
For fishing on the River Rother contact the Edenbridge Angling Club.
☎ 0737 644122

Special Interests

ARTS AND CRAFTS

The Craftsman Gallery Pottery Workshop
8 High Street, Ditchling
Manufacturer of earthenware pottery and anniversary plates. Demonstrations, pottery for sale.
☎ 0791 85246

FOOD AND DRINK

Sedlescombe Vineyard
Cripps Corner, Staplecross
The country's first organic vineyard. Traditional winemaking, working press and antique corking machine.
☎ 0580 830715

GARDENS

Haremere Hall
Etchingham
Extensive parkland with terraced gardens and a nature trail.
☎ 0580 81245

Great Dixter House and Gardens
4 miles east at Northiam
Informal gardens separated by yew hedges and original farm buildings. The Meadow Garden is of special interest in spring.
☎ 0797 253160

HISTORIC BUILDINGS

Bodiam Castle
1 mile east of Bodiam off the A229
Built in 1385 but uninhabited since the 17th century. Walls, towers and moat well-preserved; far-reaching views from the towers and battlements. Museum and audio-visual display. National Trust.
☎ 0580 830436

HISTORIC HOUSES

Great Dixter House and Gardens
Built in 1460 - a timber-framed hall-house featuring fine furniture and needlework. Family in residence.
☎ 0797 253160

Haremere Hall
Etchingham
Historic Tudor manor house.
☎ 0580 81245

MUSEUMS

Ditchling Museum
Church Lane
Former Victorian village school with
local history, domestic and farm
implements and costume. Art
collection.
☎ 0791 84744

Quarry Steam Centre
Privately-owned collection of steam
engines, open farm and crafts.
☎ 0580 830670

RAILWAYS

Kent and East Sussex Steam Railway
Tenterden Town Station, Tenterden
☎ 0580 62943 schedules
☎ 0580 65155 enquiries

Bognor Regis began as a Saxon village and developed in mediaeval times into a fishing
hamlet. In the late 1700s it grew into a fashionable seaside town. The town has many
elegant Regency and Georgian houses amongst its pleasant streets. The town had the
'Regis' part of its name added after King George V visited it in the late 1920s.

   Today Bognor Regis, with its five miles of sandy, safe beach, range of seaside
attractions and leisure facilities, is an ever popular family holiday centre.

i Belmont Street
☎ 0243 823140

Market days Monday, Wednesday,
Friday, Saturday
Population 53,175

Indoor Sports

LEISURE CENTRES

Arun Leisure Centre
Felpham Way
Sports hall, sunbed suite, squash
courts and children's games.
☎ 0243 826612

Outdoor Leisure

GOLF

Bognor Regis Golf Club ⌐₁₈
Downview Road, Felpham
Visitors welcome; accompanied by a
member at weekends.
☎ 0243 865209

Special Interests

FESTIVALS AND FAIRS

March/April
International Clown Convention

July
Carnival Week

August
International Birdman Rally – a contest
to see who can glide furthest from the
pier.

Rotary Motor Gala

FUN PARKS

Rainbow's End Circus World
Hotham Park
Waterless swimming pool, mini farm,
clowns, kiddies disco and Big-Top
shows.
☎ 0243 825255

Butlin's Southcoast World
Gloucester Road
Swimming, dancing, boating, games and
fair rides plus much more; entry with a
day pass.
☎ 0243 822445

HISTORIC HOUSES

Hotham House
Georgian mansion set in acres of public
woodland.

MUSEUMS

Bognor Regis Local History Museum
Hotham Park Lodge
200 years of local history; exhibits
contributed by local people.

71

ORNAMENTAL PARKS

Hotham Park
Woodland, flower beds, trees and grassed areas surrounding Hotham House. Children's zoo.

THEATRES

Bognor Regis Centre
Theatre, dance hall, cinema and function/conference suite. Contact the Centre's Administrative Office for details of events and hiring.
☎ 0243 865915

Water Sports

YACHTING

Bognor Regis Yacht Club
☎ 0243 865735

Felpham Yacht Club
Contact Mr Pullinger
☎ 0243 865115

Royal Pavilion, Brighton

72

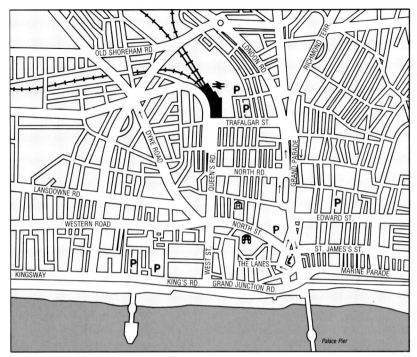

Palace Pier

Brighton, once a tiny fishing hamlet, has become one of Britain's most popular resorts. The preserved, narrow streets of the original hamlet are now called The Lanes and are lined with excellent shops, many of them antique shops.

Brighton was first recommended as a seaside resort in the mid-1700s when Doctor Russell of Lewes published a dissertation on the therapeutic value of sea bathing. Visitors began to appear in Brighton including, in 1783, the Prince of Wales, later to become King George IV. With the King's patronage Brighton became a fashionable resort as reflected by its streets of richly contrasting architectural styles – Regency terraces, late-Victorian villas and graceful Georgian streets.

Contemporary Brighton has three miles of seafront promenade and amusements, a superbly restored Victorian Palace Pier, the largest marina in Britain with a wide range of water sports facilities, theatres and a wide selection of cosmopolitan restaurants.

i Marlborough House
54 Old Steine
☎ 0273 23755

Early closing Wednesday
Population 150,000

Aerial Sports

HANG GLIDING

Sussex College of Hang Gliding
0 Crescent Road
☎ 0273 609925

Indoor Sports

ICE SKATING

Sussex Ice Rink
Queen Square
☎ 0273 24677

LEISURE CENTRES

Stanley Deason Leisure Centre
Wilson Avenue
Dry centre with facilities for racquet sports, basketball, netball, archery trampolining, skiing and more.
☎ 0273 694281

73

Withdean Sports Complex
Tongdean Lane
Tennis centre, indoor and outdoor
courts; squash courts and athletics
facilities.
☎ 0273 542100

Outdoor Leisure

FISHING

Sea Fishing
Fishing off the beach, from the marina or
from boats. Contact the Tourist
Information Centre for details.
☎ 0273 23755

GOLF

Brighton and Hove Golf Club ⛳
Dyke Road
Visitors welcome without reservation.
☎ 0273 556482

Dyke Golf Club ⛳
Dyke Road
Visitors welcome except Sunday
mornings.
☎ 0273 857296/857230

Hollingbury Park Golf Club ⛳
Ditchling Road
Visitors welcome without reservation.
☎ 0273 552010

Pyecombe Golf Club ⛳
Clayton Hill, Pyecombe
Visitors generally welcome; some
restrictions.
☎ 07918 5398

Waterhall Golf Club ⛳
Mill Road
Visitors welcome; enquire prior to visit.
☎ 0273 508658

HORSE RACING

Brighton Racecourse
1¹/₂ mile, left-handed course.
☎ 0273 682912/603580

Special Interests

ANTIQUES

The Lanes
There are many antique shops and other
specialist shops in these picturesque
streets and alleys, the oldest part of
Brighton.

AQUARIUMS

Brighton Sea Life Centre
Marine Parade
35 displays of live creatures,
multi-level viewing and audio-
visual presentations
☎ 0273 604234

ART GALLERIES

Brighton Museum and Art Gallery
Church Street
Fine 19th century Moorish-style
building containing art collections,
costume displays and local history.
☎ 0273 603005

Gardner Theatre
Sussex University Campus
This venue houses an art gallery together
with a theatre, bar and café.
☎ 0273 685861

**Rottingdean Grange Art Gallery and
Museum**
The Green, Rottingdean
Georgian house with art collection and
part of the National Toy Collection.
Exhibition also includes Rudyard
Kipling memorabilia.
☎ 0273 301004

FESTIVALS AND FAIRS

January
Holiday on Ice Show at the Brighton
Centre.

May
British Craft and Arts Fair at the
Brighton Centre.

Brighton International Festival
Old Ship Royal Escape Yacht Race at the
Old Ship Hotel.

November
London to Brighton RAC veteran car
run.

HERITAGE

Devil's Dyke
5 miles north-west of Brighton
Huge entrenchment in the South
Downs said to have been cut out by the
Devil.

HISTORIC BUILDINGS

Royal Pavilion
Old Steine
Built by Henry Holland in 1787, rebuilt
by Nash in 1820 with Chinese style
interiors, minarets and domes.
☎ 0273 603005

HISTORIC HOUSES

Preston Manor
Preston Park
Georgian manor on the site of a 13th century house with collections of silver, glass, ceramics, clocks and furniture.
☎ 0273 603005

MUSEUMS

The Barlow Collection
University of Sussex
3000 years of Chinese civilisation.
☎ 0273 678258

Booth Museum of Natural History
194 Dyke Road
Birds, butterflies and nature conservation; exhibitions.
☎ 0273 552586

Brighton Museum and Art Gallery
Displays of Art Nouveau and Art Deco furniture and decorative art; award winning Fashion Gallery; paintings; archaeology; Willett Collection of porcelain and pottery.
☎ 0273 603005

National Museum of Penny Slot Machines
Moving to Hastings 1991
Collection of vintage and antique penny-slot machines dating from 1895 until 1955, all in working order.
☎ 0273 608020

Rottingdean Grange Art Gallery and Museum
☎ 0273 301004

THEATRES

The Brighton Centre
Largest venue on south coast, seating 5000 people.
☎ 0273 202881

The Dome Complex
Historic 2000 seat concert hall set in the grounds of the Royal Pavilion.
0273 685097

Gardner Theatre
Sussex University Campus
Contemporary theatrical and musical productions. Art gallery.
☎ 0273 685861

Theatre Royal
New Road
Many famous productions.
☎ 0273 28488

RAILWAYS

Volks Electric Railway
Madeira Drive
Britain's first public electric railway, it runs for 1¼ miles along the seafront.
☎ 0273 681061

Water Sports

SWIMMING

Prince Regent Swimming Complex
Church Street
Indoor complex with pool, water chute, learner's pool, solarium and fitness studio.
☎ 0273 685692

WINDSURFING

Hove Lagoon Watersports Centre Ltd
Windsurfing and dinghy sailing tuition at all levels.
☎ 0444 892549

Sun Sports
Between Palace Pier and West Street
Courses and equipment hire available from April to October.
☎ 0273 23160

YACHT CHARTER

Brighton Marina
For details of yacht charter from the marina.
☎ 0273 693636

YACHTING

Brighton Marina Sea School
Brighton Marina
Weekend or longer cruising courses from Brighton Marina.
☎ 0273 600044

Brighton Marina Village
Largest yacht marina in Britain.
Watersports, fishing, shops, cafés and
bars.
☎ 0273 693636

Brighton Marina Yacht Club
☎ 0273 697049

Brighton Sailing Club
☎ 0273 21802

Sussex Motor Yacht Club
7 Ship Street
☎ 0273 29494

Broadstairs is a popular residential and holiday town on the north Kent coast. The
resort has several small sandy bays and the old town clusters round the fishing
harbour and pier. The town derives its name from the wide gap or 'stairs' in the cliffs.
Charles Dickens spent many summers writing his books here whilst staying at Fort
House, later re-named Bleak House after his novel of the same name.

i Pierremont Hall
67 High Street
☎ 0843 68399

Early closing Wednesday
Population 23,447

Outdoor Leisure

FISHING

Sea Fishing
Contact the Tourist Information Centre
for details.
☎ 0843 68399

GOLF

North Foreland Golf Club ⏸18
The Clubhouse, Convent Road
Two 18-hole courses, visitors with a
handicap certificate welcome on
weekdays and weekend afternoons.
☎ 0843 62140/69628

HORSE RIDING

Ditchling Common Stud
Ditchling Common
Hacking on common and downland,
general instruction, training for
competitions and career students, liver
and courses.
☎ 0444 236678/871900

76

St Stephen's College Riding School
North Foreland
Pony club; basic instruction in riding, jumping and livery.
☎ 0843 62254/65294

TENNIS

Memorial Recreation Ground
6 tennis courts.
☎ 0843 61283

Special Interests

FESTIVALS AND FAIRS

June
Dickens Festival – contact the Tourist Information Centre for details.

August
Carnival
Folk Week
Water Gala

HISTORIC BUILDINGS

North Foreland Lighthouse
1¹/₂ miles north of Broadstairs
Good views of ships entering and leaving the Thames estuary.

Crampton Tower
Victorian railway engines in 19th century tower.

The Pavilion
Harbour Street

St Peter's Church
12th century church.

York Gate
16th century architecture.

HISTORIC HOUSES

Bleak House
House where Dickens lived while writing *David Copperfield*. The house is named after another of Dickens' books.

MUSEUMS

Crampton Tower Museum
High Street
General railway exhibits and items relating to engineer T R Crampton.
☎ 0843 62078

Dickens House Museum
2 Victoria Parade
House featured in *David Copperfield* now contains Dickens' letters and possessions.
☎ 0843 62224

Water Sports

YACHTING

Broadstairs Sailing Club
☎ 0843 61373

KENT / **Bromley** / KENT

Bromley, once a market town, is now an outer suburb of London. It is fortunate in retaining many commons and country parks including an extensive area of natural woodland at Petts Wood. In Bromley High Street there is a plaque commemorating the site of the birthplace of H G Wells, the science fiction writer. The area has excellent sports facilities including the National Sports Centre at Crystal Palace and there are several notable golf courses here.

i Central Library
High Street
☎ 081 313 1113

Market day Thursday
Population 294,526

Indoor Sports

BADMINTON

National Sports Centre
Crystal Palace
☎ 081 778 0131

LEISURE CENTRES

Beckenham Leisure Centre
☎ 081 650 0233

Bromley Sports Hall
Stockwell Road, Kentish Lane
☎ 081 313 4300

National Sports Centre
Crystal Palace
☎ 081 778 0131

Walnuts Sport Centre
Orpington
☎ 0689 870533

SQUASH

Squash can be played at any of the leisure centres listed above.

Multi-Activity Holidays

MULTI-ACTIVITY CENTRES

The Field Study Centre
Scadbury Park Estate
Educational holidays and field studies.
☎ 081 302 7496

Outdoor Leisure

CYCLING

Crystal Palace to Bromley Cycle Route
Contact the Tourist Information Centre.
☎ 081 313 1113

National Sports Centre
Crystal Palace
Cycling track.
☎ 081 778 0131

FISHING

Coarse Fishing
There are many venues for good fishing including Keston Ponds and Crystal Palace Lake. For information and permits contact the National Rivers Authority at Vale Road, Tonbridge.
☎ 0732 838858

GOLF

Beckenham Place Park Golf Club ⚐
Beckenham Hill Road, Beckenham
Set in parkland; visitors welcome on weekdays but booking is required for weekends.
☎ 081 658 5374

Bromley Golf Club ⚐
Magpie Hall Lane
Municipal parkland course.
☎ 081 462 7014/8001

Chislehurst Golf Club ⚐
Camden Place, Chislehurst
Visitors welcome during the week but must be with a member at weekends.
☎ 081 467 6798

Magpie Hall Lane Municipal Golf Club ⚐
Magpie Hall Lane
A flat course suitable for beginners.
☎ 081 462 7014

Shortlands Golf Club ⚐
Meadow Road, Shortlands
☎ 081 460 2471

Sidcup Golf Club ⚐
7 Hurst Road, Sidcup
Visitors welcome on weekdays without reservation.
☎ 081 300 2150

Sundridge Park Golf Club ⚐
Garden Road, off Plaistow Lane
Two 18-hole courses, East and West, set in wooded parkland. Visitors with a handicap certificate welcome, weekdays only.
☎ 081 460 5540 Pro Shop

TENNIS

Bromley Sports Hall
Stockwell Close, Kentish Lane
☎ 081 313 4300

WALKING AND RAMBLING

There are many walks and rambling routes in the Bromley area, including several suitable for the elderly and disabled.

Cuckoo Wood Trail
High Elms Park

Jubilee Country Park
☎ 081 460 8790

The Nash Circular Walk
☎ 081 460 8790

West Wickham Town and Country Walk
☎ 081 460 8790

Special Interests

ANTIQUES

Antica
Rear of 35–41 High Street
☎ 081 464 7661

COUNTRY PARKS

There are many country parks and commons around Bromley including Keston Common, Hayes Common, High Broom Woods, Harvington Estate and Darrick Wood.

Chislehurst Common
☎ 081 467 1886

Crystal Palace Park
Woodlands, meadows and life-size
dinosaur models.
☎ 081 778 7148

High Elms Estate
Nature walk, cabin and picnic sites.

Jubilee Country Park
☎ 081 460 8790

Petts Wood
An extensive area of natural woodland,
with a memorial to William Willett,
who introduced British Summer Time.

FESTIVALS AND FAIRS

St Giles' Fair
Held annually at St Giles' Parish
Church. Contact the Tourist
Information Centre for details.

GARDENS

The Maze
Crystal Palace Park
One of the largest mazes in the country,
constructed using hornbeam hedges. The
Italian Garden and the Vale at the park
are also interesting.
☎ 081 778 7148

HERITAGE

Caesar's Well
Keston Common
Discovered in Roman times, – the head
waters of the River Ravensbourne fitted
out as a cold bath in the 18th century.

Chislehurst Caves
Old Hill, Chislehurst
Chalk mines dating back to Roman
times; used as a smugglers' store
and as the largest air raid shelter in
southern England.
☎ 081 467 3264

HISTORIC BUILDINGS

Bromley College
Founded in 1666 to house the widows of
clergymen.

The Free Watermen's and Lightermen's
Almshouses
Penge
Built in 1840 to provide houses for
retired watermen and lightermen or
their widows.

St Giles the Abbot Parish Church
Farnborough
Home of the St Giles' Fair founded in
1220 and still held annually.

St John's Parish Church
West Wickham
A mediaeval building with many
interesting features.

The Priory
Orpington
A pre-Reformation rectory house dating
back to 1270 and the home of the
Rectors of Orpington, now a local
meeting place and museum.
☎ 0689 831551

The Rawlins Almshouses
Beckenham
One of the oldest surviving buildings in
the town.

Scadbury Estate
Dating back to Saxon times and
occupied by the Walsingham family
since 1424.

HISTORIC HOUSES

Camden Place
Built in 1609 and once the home of
Napoleon III.

Down House
Formerly the home of Charles Darwin,
now owned by the Royal College of
Surgeons.

The Palace
Home of the Bishops of Rochester until
1845 and now part of the Civic Centre.

Sundridge Park
18th century mansion built under the
direction of Nash.

MUSEUMS

Bromley Museum
The Priory, Church Hill, Orpington
☎ 0689 31551

Down House
Museum dedicated to Charles Darwin.
☎ 0689 859119

The Priory
Orpington
☎ 0689 831551

NATURAL HISTORY

Crystal Palace Tree Trail
Crystal Palace Park
☎ 081 778 7148

High Elms Nature Reserve
☎ 081 460 8790

Kelsey Park
Off Beckenham High Street
Aviary and wildfowl reserve. Floral
displays.
☎ 081 650 8694

Scadbury Park Nature Reserve
Nature trail.
☎ 081 464 3333

ORNAMENTAL PARKS

Church House Gardens
Off the High Street
Flower gardens and lakes.

Priory Gardens
Orpington High Street
Lakeside setting and floral displays.

THEATRES

The Bromley Little Theatre
☎ 081 460 3047

Churchill Theatre
High Street
☎ 081 460 6677/5838

Crystal Palace Park
Open-air concert bowl.
☎ 081 778 7148

ZOOS

Crystal Palace Park
Assorted animals and birds.
☎ 081 778 7184

Water Sports

CANOEING

Beckenham Leisure Centre
☎ 081 650 0233

SWIMMING

Beckenham Leisure Centre
☎ 081 650 0233

Beckenham Road Baths
☎ 081 650 0233

Darrick Wood Pool
☎ 0689 857021

National Sports Centre
Crystal Palace
☎ 081 778 0131

Walnuts Sport Centre
Orpington
☎ 0689 70533

West Wickham Pools
☎ 081 777 5686

Burwash

Burwash is situated along a ridge between the Rivers Rother and Dudwell. This attractive village was a centre for the Sussex iron industry from the 16th to the 18th century and retains many period buildings. Rudyard Kipling had his home here at Bateman's; it is now a National Trust property. A visit to the Burwash area should include a tour of the follies of 'Mad Jack' Fuller, a local character of the early 19th century.

Special Interests

HISTORIC HOUSES

Bateman's
Built in 1634 and once owned by an iron master. Rudyard Kipling's home for over 30 years, the house was given to the National Trust by his wife. Working mill in grounds dates back to the 12th century.
☎ 0435 882302

HISTORIC BUILDINGS

Mad Jack Fuller's Mausoleum
South of Burwash at Brightling
Huge pyramid in the churchyard which Jack had built in 1810, 24 years before his death. An eccentric English gentleman, an MP and collector of works by Turner – he saved Bodiam Castle from demolition. He also built the 65-foot 'Brightling Needle', a fake church tower constructed for a bet.

THEATRES

Bateman's
Open-air theatre during summer.

Camberley, in north Surrey, has grown around the staff houses of the nearby Sandhurst Military Academy, built here in 1807. The town has become increasingly urbanised yet retains a wide stretch of open country to the east – Bagshot Heath.

Early closing Wednesday
Population 45,716

Aerial Sports

FLYING

Blackbushe School of Flying
Blackbushe Airport
☎ 0252 870999

Three Counties Aero Club
Blackbushe Airport
☎ 0252 872152

Indoor Sports

LEISURE CENTRES

Arena Leisure Centre
Grand Avenue
Sports hall, health suite, swimming,
☎ 0276 28787

Outdoor Leisure

GOLF

Camberley Heath Golf Club ⛳18
Golf Drive, Portsmouth Road
Wooded undulating heathland, guests of members and societies only.
☎ 0276 23258

Pennyhill Park Country Club ⛳9
College Ride, Bagshot
Visitors welcome by appointment.
☎ 0276 71774

Special Interests

ANTIQUES

The Antique House
47 London Road
☎ 0276 26412

COUNTRY PARKS

Lightwater Country Park
North-east of Camberley off the M3
Environmental interpretive heathland visitor centre.
☎ 0276 51605

MUSEUMS

Royal Army Ordnance Corps Museum
Blackdown Barracks, Deepcut
History of the Royal Army Ordnance Corps up to the present day.
☎ 0252 24431 extn 5515

Staff College Museum
London Road
History of staff officers in the Army. By appointment only.
☎ 0276 63344 extn 2602

Surrey Heath Museum
Surrey Heath House, Knoll Road
History of the area and heathland habitat; exhibitions.
☎ 0276 686252

THEATRES

Civic Hall
Knoll Road
Varied entertainment programme.
☎ 0276 26978

Water Sports

SWIMMING

Arena Leisure Centre
☎ 0276 28787

Canterbury Cathedral

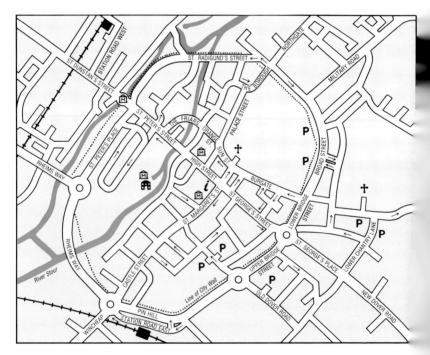

The pleasant city of Canterbury is situated on the banks of the River Stour among
gardens, meadows, orchards and chalky hills. Originally an Iron Age settlement, i
became the centre of Christianity in England after the arrival in 597 of St Augusti
who became the first archbishop of England. Its magnificent 11th century cathedr
was the scene of the martyrdom of St Thomas Becket. Long, reasonably-preserv
stretches of the town walls survive, and tall overhanging houses can be seen in t
lanes leading to the cathedral's main entrance. Mediaeval buildings and narro
alleyways conjure up vivid images of life in the Middle Ages.

i 34 St Margarets Street
☎ 0277 766567

Market days Wednesday, Saturday
Early closing Thursday
Population 36,507

Aerial Sports

MICROLIGHT FLYING

Kent Microlight and Aircraft Club
Contact John Carpenter.
☎ 0227 452439

South East Microlight Aircraft Centre
Gobery Hill Cottage, Sandwich Hill,
Wingham
☎ 0227 720400

Multi-Activity Holidays

SPECIAL INTEREST CENTRES

British School of Falconry
Stelling Minnis
Beginners and advanced birds of prey
management courses.
☎ 0227 87575

Summer Academy
University of Kent
Week-long study holidays on the
countryside, arts and literature and
heritage subjects.
☎ 0227 470402

Outdoor Leisure

CRICKET

Kent County Cricket Club
St Lawrence Ground, Old Dover Road
☎ 0227 456886

FALCONRY

British School of Falconry
☎ 0227 87575

FISHING

Coarse Fishing
Fishing on the River Stour. For
information and permits contact the
National Rivers Authority.
☎ 0732 838858
☎ 0323 762691

GOLF

Broome Park Golf and Country Club
The Broome Park Estate, Barham
☎ 0227 831701

Canterbury Golf Club ▶ß
Scotland Hills, Littlebourne Road
Visitors welcome without reservation.
☎ 0227 453532/462865

HORSE RIDING

Chaucer Riding and Livery Stables
6 miles south-west off the A2068 at
Waltham
Instructional holidays, jumping and a
riding club.
☎ 0227 70297

Oathill Farm Riding Centre
Pound Lane, Molash
Treks, treasure hunts, jumping and
gymkhana.
☎ 0233 74573

WALKING AND RAMBLING

North Downs Way
141 miles from Farnham across the
North Downs with beautiful views. In
places it follows the ancient mediaeval
Pilgrim's Way which ran from
Winchester to Canterbury.

Special Interests

ANTIQUES

Acorn Antiques
19 Best Lane
☎ 0227 450171

ART GALLERIES

The Graphics Gallery
University of Kent
Gallery of cartoons and caricatures.
☎ 0227 764000 extn 3127/8

**Royal Museum, Art Gallery and Buffs
Regimental Museum**
Paintings by local artists.
☎ 0227 452747

ARTS AND CRAFTS

Summer Academy
School of Continuing Education, The
University
Holiday study programmes include
countryside and arts subjects.
☎ 0227 470402

FARM PARKS

Parsonage Farm Rural Heritage Centre
10 miles south, just off the B2065 at
North Elmham
Working family farm with historical
displays and exhibitions.
☎ 0303 840766

FESTIVALS AND FAIRS

April
Chaucer Festival at Canterbury
Cathedral.
☎ 0227 762862

August
Cricket Week

October
Arts Festival

December
Carol service in Canterbury Cathedral.

FOOD AND DRINK

Elham Valley Vineyards
Breach, Barham
☎ 0227 831266

St Nicholas of Ash Vineyard and Winery
Moat Farm, Moat Lane, Ash
☎ 0304 812670

Staple Vineyards
Church Farm, Staple
7-acre vineyard including a small
collection of old farm implements.
☎ 0304 812571

Theobalds Barn Cider
Heronsgate Farm, Stourmouth
Fruit grown, pressed and distilled on
farm for natural cider and apple juice.
Prior notice required.
☎ 0227 722275

GARDENS

Gooderstone Park
Wingham
Walled, woodland and rose gardens.
☎ 0304 840218

GUIDED TOURS

Canterbury Guild of Guides
Arnett House, Hawks Lane
☎ 0227 459779

HERITAGE

St Augustine's Abbey
Ruins of the abbey and monastery
found in AD 598; includes both Saxon
and Norman work; small museum.
☎ 0227 767345

HISTORIC BUILDINGS

Canterbury Cathedral
The mother church of the Church of
England and one of the finest cathedrals
in Britain. Begun in 1067, gutted by fire
in 1174 and then rebuilt to its present
design. A place of pilgrimage for 350
years until Thomas Becket's Shrine
was destroyed by Henry VIII in 1538.
Exquisite mediaeval stained glass; the
largest Norman crypt in Britain; the
tombs of Henry IV and the Black Prince,
and the 12 century choir and 14th
century screen add to its exceptional
beauty and interest. Frequent events
and exhibitions.
☎ 0227 762862

Cathedral gateway

Detail from Canterbury Cathedral

Poor Priests Hospital
Stour Street
Now the Canterbury Heritage Museum
14th century hospice with the history
Canterbury and a 'time walk'
experience.
☎ 0227 452747

MUSEUMS

Canterbury Centre
St Alphege Lane
12th century church with local history displays.
☎ 0227 457009

Canterbury Heritage Museum
Stour Street
Mediaeval building. Historical artefacts dating back 2000 years are displayed.
☎ 0227 452747

Canterbury Pilgrims Way
St Margarets Street
Audio-visual experience of Chaucer's *Canterbury Tales* based in St Margaret's Church.
☎ 0227 454888

Ethnic Doll and Toy Museum
Moving to Whitstable 1991
Toys and dolls from all over the world.
☎ 0227 471032

Royal Museum, Art Gallery and Buffs Regimental Museum
18 High Street
History and archaeology, paintings by local artists and local regiment museum.
☎ 0227 452747

St Augustine's Abbey
☎ 0227 767345

West Gate Museum
St Peters Street
Fortified gatehouse, a prison for some time, containing military exhibits.
☎ 0227 452747

THEATRES

Marlowe Theatre
Accommodates drama, opera, pantomime and dance productions.
☎ 0227 767246

Gulbenkien Theatre
University of Kent
☎ 0227 769075

WILDLIFE PARKS

Blean Bird Park
Honey Hill, Blean
Bird collection; largest collection of parrots on show in the UK. Pet's corner, café, shop.
☎ 0227 471666

Wingham Bird Park
Rusham Road, Wingham
Waterfowl and aviaries.
☎ 0227 720836

ZOOS

Howletts Zoo
3 miles south of Canterbury off the A2 at Bekesbourne
Tigers, elephants, monkeys and the world's largest gorilla colony in 300 acres. Cafés, gift shops and picnic areas.
☎ 0227 721286

Water Sports

BOAT TRIPS

Reneroy IV River Trips
Off the A28 at Upstreet
☎ 0227 86302

CANOEING

Riverside Outdoor Education
Kingsmead Road
☎ 0227 470038

anterbury town centre

Once a small, sleepy, upland village, Caterham came to life when the railway arrived in 1856. It has now grown to fill the whole valley and some of the surrounding downs. Gravelly Hill lies to the south of the town; it rises to 778 feet, giving good views and access to the ancient Pilgrim's Way.

Market day Thursday
Early closing Wednesday

Adventure Sports

SHOOTING

Copthorne Gun Club
Off the A22
☎ 081 660 4702

Aerial Sports

GLIDING

Surrey Hills Gliding Club
Kenley Airfield, Kenley
☎ 0737 554319 Secretary

Indoor Sports

LEISURE CENTRES

De Stafford School
Burntwood Lane
☎ 0883 722000

Oxted County School Sports Hall
Blue House Lane, Oxted
☎ 0883 722000

Outdoor Leisure

GOLF

North Downs Golf Club ♟
North Down Road, Woldingham
Visitors welcome.
☎ 0883 853298

HORSE RIDING

Beechwood Riding School
Hillboxes Farm, Marden Park, Woldingham
General instruction for adults and children; long and short term courses, general purpose schooling and hacking in parkland.
☎ 0883 342266

Woldingham Equestrian Centre
South Fields Road, Woldingham
Hacking in the North Downs, general instruction, schooling and livery.
☎ 0883 853034

WALKING AND RAMBLING

North Downs Way
Gravelly Hill
Passes south of the town on the route of the ancient mediaeval Pilgrim's Way. Good views.

Special Interests

FARM PARKS

Godstone Farm
Tilburstow Hill Road, Godstone
Children's farm; climb-in pens; adventure playground.
☎ 0883 742546

MUSEUMS

East Surrey Museum
1 Stafford Road
Local history and a programme of exhibitions.
☎ 0883 340275

Water Sports

WINDSURFING

Mercers Park Windsurfing
Nutfield Marsh Road, Merstham
RYA Levels 1 and 2 instruction available.
☎ 0737 644288

Chatham

Situated on the estuary of the River Medway, Chatham has long been an important port with a naval dockyard. The first of its docks was founded by Henry VIII, burnt down in 1667 and rebuilt at the end of the 17th century to become England's first naval base. Several interesting 18th century houses can be seen at the core of the Royal Naval Dockyard. Dickens spent part of his childhood here and mentions the area in his works.

i Eastgate Cottage
High Street
Rochester
☎ 0634 843666

Early closing Wednesday
Population 63,000

Aerial Sports

FLYING

Rochester Aviation Flying Club
Rochester Airport
☎ 0634 816340

Outdoor Leisure

FISHING

Coarse Fishing
For information and permits contact the National Rivers Authority.
☎ 0732 771030

Capstone Country Park
Capstone Park
☎ 0634 812196

ropellor, The Historic Dockyard

GOLF

Chatham Golf Centre
Street End Road
Golf driving range.
☎ 0634 848925

HORSE RIDING

The Royal Engineers Saddle Club
Royal School of Military Engineering,
Brompton Barracks
☎ 0634 844555

Special Interests

COUNTRY PARKS

Capstone Farm Country Park
Capstone Road
Nature trails; lake and bridleway; picnic sites and disabled facilities.
☎ 0634 812916

MUSEUMS

Fort Amherst
Napoleonic fort with 14 acres of batteries, bastions, redoubts and tunnels. A taste of life in an underground stronghold as experienced by soldiers and prisoners.
☎ 0634 847747

The Historic Dockyard
80-acre dockyard with shops, working trade displays and audio-visual presentations. 'Wooden Walls' tells the story of building the British fighting ship.
☎ 0634 812551

Old Brook Pumping Station
Solomon's Road
Pumping station, built in 1929, with original working machinery.
☎ 0634 42059

THEATRES

Medway Arts Centre
Old Town Hall
☎ 0634 842984/829306

YACHTING

Medway Sea School
The Historic Dockyard
Holiday and weekend sailing courses and
holidays.
☎ 0634 402518

Water Sports

BOAT TRIPS

Kingswear Castle Excursions Ltd
Chatham Historic Dockyard
Trips aboard a coal-fired paddle steamer
from Strood Pier. Afternoon cruises, jazz,
private hire from May to October.
☎ 0634 827648

Winter Sports

SKIING

The Alpine Ski Centre
Capstone Country Park Grounds,
Capstone Road
200-metre by 45-metre slope, two lifts,
floodlit. Instruction available.
☎ 0634 827979

SURREY · **Chertsey** · SURREY

This pleasant, old-fashioned town features a charming seven-arch, 18th century
bridge spanning the River Thames. Amongst its old buildings are the quaint, partly
17th century George Inn, and Curfew House built in 1729. The church houses a
curfew bell which commemorates Blanche Heriot, who saved her lover's life. The
unfortunate man would have been executed at curfew, but Blanche silenced the bell
by hanging on its clapper until he was reprieved. There are good views to the north-
west from St Anne's Hill.

Aerial Sports

FLYING

Fairoaks Flying Club
Fairoaks Airport, Chobham
☎ 0276 858075

Water Sports

BOAT TRIPS

French Brothers
Scheduled sailings between Runnymede,
Windsor, Staines, Chertsey and
Hampton Court.
☎ 0753 851900/862933

Special Interests

MUSEUMS

Chertsey Museum
33 Windsor Street, Chertsey
History and archaeology of Runnymede;
costume collection.
☎ 0932 565764

RAILWAYS

Great Cockcrow Railway
Hardwick Lane, Lyne
Miniature railway with unique
signalling system.
☎ 0932 228950 Sundays

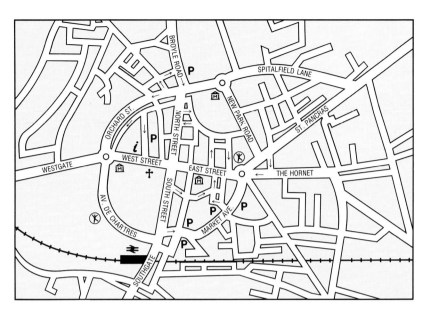

Situated between the sea and the South Downs, the City of Chichester retains its original Roman layout of four main streets enclosed within a city wall. Chichester boasts a wealth of interesting architecture including unspoilt Georgian buildings, ancient churches and a lovely Norman cathedral.

i St Peter's Market
West Street
☎ 0243 775888

Market days Wednesday, Saturday
Early closing Thursday
Population 27,241

Aerial Sports

FLYING

Goodwood Aerodrome
☎ 0243 774656

PARACHUTING

Flying Tigers Skydiving Centre
Goodwood Airfield
☎ 0243 533444

Indoor Sports

LEISURE CENTRES

Southern Leisure Centre
Vinnetrow Road
☎ 0243 787715

Westgate
Avenue de Chartres
Sports hall, squash courts, conditioning room, keep fit, bar and terrace, pools.
☎ 0243 785651

Multi-Activity Holidays

SPECIAL INTEREST CENTRES

The Earnley Concourse
Earnley
☎ 0243 670392

Outdoor Leisure

BIRDWATCHING

The Earnley Concourse
☎ 0243 670392

FISHING

Coarse Fishing
For information and permits contact the National Rivers Authority.
☎ 0323 762691

Chichester Canal Society
Details from J Cooper, 'Jaspers', East
Wittering.
☎ 0243 671051

Chichester and District Angling Society
☎ 0243 866663

Peckhams Copse
Trout and coarse fishing on gravel pits
Enquiries to the Manager of the
Southern Leisure Centre.
☎ 0243 787715

Chichester Cathedral

Game Fishing

Furnace Park Trout Fishery
☎ 0435 830298/830151

GOLF

Goodwood Golf Club 🏌
Goodwood
Visitors welcome by prior arrangement,
handicap certificate required for
weekends.
☎ 0243 785012

Selsey Golf Club 🏌
Off the B2145 at Selsey
Visitors generally welcome.
☎ 0444 414866

HORSE RACING

Goodwood Racecourse
The racecourse is part of the Goodwood
House Estate. A right-handed, loop
course it hosts 18 flat racing days each
year. Renowned for its summer race
season – 'Glorious Goodwood',
strawberries, champagne and fine racing.
☎ 0243 774107

HORSE RIDING

Zara Stud and Training Centres
Highleigh Road, Sidlesham
General instruction in riding and
jumping; convalescent treatment and
western-style riding.
☎ 0243 641 662

Special Interests

ANTIQUES

Bosham Antiques
Delling Lane, Bosham
☎ 0243 572005

ARTS AND CRAFTS

Bosham Walk
Bosham Lane, Bosham
Arcade of varied craft shops with
craftsmen at work and items for sale.

Geraldine St Aubyn Hubbard
Rosebrook, Farm Lane, Nutbourne
Handwoven silk and wool cloth for
scarves and clothes.
☎ 0243 377372

FESTIVALS AND FAIRS

February
Music Festival

July
Chichester Gala
☎ 0243 773652

Chichester Festivities
☎ 0243 776003

July/August
Glorious Goodwood
Goodwood International Dressage

August
Royal Military Police March

FOOD AND DRINK

Chilsdown Vineyard
Old Station House, Singleton
13-acre vineyard and winery.
☎ 0243 63398

GARDENS

Apuldram Roses
Apuldram Lane, Dell Quay
Specialist rose nursery with over 300
rose varieties in mature garden.
☎ 0243 785769

Earnley Butterflies and Gardens
133 Almodington Lane, Earnley
17 theme gardens. Tropical butterflies
and birds and a small animal farm.
☎ 0243 512637

West Dean Gardens
West Dean
Mainly informal gardens established in
1622. Ancient trees, pergola and
Victorian greenhouses.
☎ 0243 63303

GUIDED TOURS

Regular and group tours available.
Contact the Tourist Information Centre
for details.
☎ 0243 775888

HERITAGE

City Walls
Various locations – this was one of the
earliest walled towns.

Fishbourne Roman Palace and Museum
Salthill Road, Fishbourne
Remains of the largest Roman residences
ever excavated in Britain, probably the
palace of King Cogidubnus. Impressive
mosaics.
☎ 0243 785859

HISTORIC BUILDINGS

Bishops Palace
South-west of the Cathedral
The building has a mediaeval kitchen
and a fine wall painting of the
Winchester school.
☎ 0243 782595

Chichester Cathedral
The Royal Chantry, The Cloisters
Construction began in 1075 at the behest
of William the Conqueror. Richard of
Chichester lies buried here, as well as
the composer Gustav Holst. Large art
collection from Roman stone carvings
to famous modern paintings, sculpture
and tapestries.
☎ 0243 782595

St Mary's Hospital
St Martins Square
13th century almshouses.
☎ 0243 783377

HISTORIC HOUSES

Goodwood House
Goodwood
18th century house, home of the Dukes
of Richmond, antique furniture, fine
porcelain and painting collections. Set in
wooded parkland.
☎ 0243 774107

Pallant House
North Pallant
Queen Anne town house with
collections of porcelain, paintings and
sculpture.
☎ 0243 774557

MUSEUMS

Chichester District Museum
29 Little London
Geology, archaeology and social history
exhibits.
☎ 0243 784683

Fishbourne Roman Palace and Museum
☎ 0243 785859

Guildhall Museum
Priory Park, Priory Road
13th century Greyfriars Church with
archaeology of Chichester and
surrounding area.
☎ 0243 784683

Mechanical Music and Doll Collection
Church Road, Parfield
☎ 0243 785421

Museum of D-Day Aviation
Manor Farm, Apuldram
The aviation story of D-Day.
☎ 0243 572967

The Red Cap Museum
Roissillon Barracks, Broyle Road
☎ 0243 786311

Tangmere Military Aviation Museum
Tangmere Airfield
Battle of Britain airfield. Aircraft, maps,
photographs medals and uniforms on
display.
☎ 0243 775223

Weald and Downland Open Air Museum
Singleton
Collection of rescued historic buildings
including houses, barns, a market hall
and a mill dating from mediaeval times.
☎ 0243 63 348

THEATRES

Festival Theatre
Oaklands Park
☎ 0243 781312

WILDLIFE PARKS

Earnley Butterflies and Gardens
133 Almodington Lane, Earnley
Butterfly, rabbit and bird
sanctuary; theme gardens.
☎ 0243 512637

Water Sports

BOAT TRIPS

Chichester Harbour Water Tours
Peter Adams, 9 Cawley Road
1½ hour cruises with full commentary.
☎ 0243 786418 talking timetable

SWIMMING

Westgate Centre
Avenue de Chartres
Three swimming pools and a water slide.
☎ 0243 785651

WINDSURFING

Chichester Sailing Centre
☎ 0243 512557

YACHTING

Chichester Sailing Centre
Chichester Marina
Cruising and flotilla training on
luxurious American yachts.
☎ 0243 512557

**The Solent Coastal and Offshore Sailing
School**
Archipelagoes, South Mundham
Instructional cruising courses. Group
bookings available.
☎ 0243 262724

Popular with antique seekers, this attractive village includes a square of half-timbered houses and an interesting 15th century flint church.

Early closing Thursday
Population 1500

Outdoor Leisure

FALCONRY

Chilham Castle Gardens
Birds of prey demonstrations.
☎ 0227 730319

Special Interests

ANTIQUES

Chilham Square

Chilham Square
Many of the delightful houses in
Chilham have now been converted to
antique shops.

GARDENS

Chilham Castle Gardens
Jacobean terraced gardens overlooking
the Stour valley. Birds of prey
demonstrations, jousting at weekends.
☎ 0227 730319

HERITAGE

Julieberrie's Grave
Long barrow near the banks of the Stour,
good views.

HISTORIC BUILDINGS

Chilham Castle
Jacobean mansion; octagonal Norman
keep.
☎ 0227 730319

Cobham

Cobham has been considerably redeveloped yet retains many pleasant old buildings. Queen Matilda, who died in 1118, is reputed to have built Cobham Bridge after one of her ladies drowned while attempting to cross the ford.

Outdoor Leisure

GOLF

Fairmile Driving Range
Fairmile Hotel
Driving range only.

Silvermere Golf Club
Redhill Road
☎ 0932 867275

HORSE RIDING

Cobham Manor Riding Centre
Water Lane, Thurnham
General instruction, livery and hacking.
☎ 0622 38497

Lower Farm Riding and Livery Stables
Stoke Road, Stoke d'Abernon Livery, hacking, general RDA instruction.
☎ 0932 867545

Special Interests

GARDENS

Painshill Park
Portsmouth Road
Restored 18th century landscaped park featuring follies, grotto, bridge and waterwheel.
☎ 0932 864674/868113

HISTORIC BUILDINGS

Chatley Heath Semaphore Tower
Ex-Admiralty Naval Station. Stunning roof-top views. 20 minute well-marked walk to the tower.
☎ 0932 862762

Church Stile House
Church Street
A fine example of ancient overhung Surrey timberwork.

St Mary Magdalene Church
13th century church with fine mediaeval brasses.

MUSEUMS

Cobham Bus Museum
Redhill Road
Private collection of buses dating from the 1930's to the present.
☎ 0932 864078

Crawley

Set in magnificent countryside offering many fine walks, Crawley is a predominantly modern town with a wide range of leisure amenities. There are several attractive old buildings in the High Street.

Market day Saturday
Early closing Wednesday
Population 80,726

Indoor Sports

BADMINTON

Bewbush Leisure Centre
Breezehurst Drive
☎ 0293 546477

LEISURE CENTRES

Crawley Leisure Centre
Haslett Avenue
Multi purpose halls, fitness unit, running track and soccer pitches.
☎ 0293 537431

SQUASH

Bewbush Leisure Centre
Breezehurst Drive
☎ 0293 546477

Crawley Leisure Centre
☎ 0293 537431

TEN PIN BOWLING

Crawley Bowl
High Street
☎ 0293 527977

Outdoor Leisure

FISHING

Coarse Fishing

Isfield Mill Pond
☎ 0293 528744

Tilgate Park
Fishing available on the lake.
☎ 0293 528744

GOLF

Copthorne Golf Club ⛳
Borers Arms Road, Copthorne
Flat wooded course. Visitors welcome
weekdays without reservation; after
2 pm on weekends.
☎ 0342 712033

Cottesmore Golf Club ⛳
Buchan Hill, Pease Pottage
Undulating parkland course. Visitors
welcome except before 11 am weekends.
☎ 0293 528256

Tilgate Forest Golf Club
Titmus Drive, Tilgate
Visitors welcome; must book at
weekends.
☎ 0293 530103

TENNIS

Crawley Leisure Centre
All-weather courts.
☎ 0293 537431

Langley Green Playing Fields
Cherry Lane
☎ 0293 520489

Southgate Playing Fields
Southgate Avenue
☎ 0293 537086

WALKING AND RAMBLING

Worth Way
Six-mile walk from Three Bridges,
Crawley to East Grinstead along a
disused railway line.
☎ 0444 458166

Special Interests

ANTIQUES

Hickmet Southways Ltd
Southways Lowfield Heath
☎ 0293 531616

COUNTRY PARKS

Buchan Country Park
2 miles west of Crawley off the A264
Woodland surrounding two ponds.
Visitor centre.
☎ 0293 542088

Tilgate Park
Titmus Drive
400 acres of woodland, lakes and
ornamental gardens.
☎ 0293 528744

GARDENS

Nymans Garden
Handcross
Walled garden with Italian fountain,
sunken garden and many rare and
beautiful trees, shrubs and plants
collected from all over the world.
☎ 0444 400321

HISTORIC BUILDINGS

Isfield Mill
Outskirts of Crawley
Restored by volunteers.
☎ 0293 528744

ORNAMENTAL PARKS

Memorial Gardens
Town centre

THEATRES

The Hawth
Hawth Avenue
☎ 0293 553636

ZOOS

Gatwick Zoo
Charlwood
10 acres with assorted animals, birds and
butterflies.
☎ 0293 862312

Water Sports

WINDSURFING

Tilgate Park
☎ 0293 528744

Crowborough is a country town and important golfing centre with a wealth of Victorian architecture at its centre. There are panoramic views across Ashdown Forest from Beacon Hill.

Early closing Wednesday
Population 18,200

Indoor Sports

LEISURE CENTRES

Goldsmiths Leisure Centre
Eridge Road
Fitness room, squash and badminton courts, solarium, bar.
☎ 0892 665488

SQUASH

Crowborough Tennis and Squash Club
☎ 0892 652618

Goldsmiths Leisure Centre
☎ 0892 665488

Multi-Activity Holidays

SPECIAL INTEREST CENTRES

The English Language and Equestrian Centre
Friars Gate Farm
General instruction, residential holiday courses, liveries, shows, English language courses.
☎ 0892 661195

Outdoor Leisure

CAMPING AND CARAVANNING

Crowborough Caravan and Camping Site
Goldsmiths Leisure Centre, Eridge Road
10 pitches on a secluded site close to a fully equipped sports centre.
☎ 089 26 64827

FISHING

Coarse Fishing
Crowborough & District Angling Association. Membership enquiries.
Crowborough Tackle, Whitehill Road.

GOLF

Crowborough Beacon Golf Club ⛳18
Growel Hill, Addington
Visitors welcome; weekends and Bank Holidays accompanied by a member.
☎ 0892 661511

Haywards Heath Golf Club ⛳18
$1\frac{1}{4}$ miles north of Haywards Heath off the B2028
Visitors welcome; telephone ahead.
☎ 0444 414457

TENNIS

Crowborough Tennis and Squash Club
☎ 0892 652618

Wolfe Recreation Ground
Blackness Road

WALKING AND RAMBLING

High Weald Walkers
Crowborough Branch of Ramblers Association. Contact Mr T Collyer, Flinders, Church Road.
☎ 0892 662108

Special Interests

COUNTRY PARKS

Jarvis Brook Country Park
Osborne Road/Tollwood Road
Wildlife, walking.

FOOD AND DRINK

Castle Hill Farm
Rotherfield
Cheese makers; visitors welcome to see
the cheese being made. Telephone before
a visit.
☎ 0892 852207

FOREST PARKS

Ashdown Forest
Information Barn off the A22 Wych
Cross to Colemans Hatch road
Woodland and heathland, wildlife and
walks in open country immortalised in
the map of Pooh Country; part of the
High Weald Area of Outstanding
Natural Beauty.

MUSEUMS

**Conan Doyle (Crowborough)
Establishment**
Memorabilia. Tours arranged: contact
Mr M Payne.
☎ 0892 663021

Water Sports

SWIMMING

Goldsmiths Swimming Pool
Eridge Road
☎ 0892 665488

Cuckfield has a delightful old High Street, magnificent church and picturesque
cottages. Cuckfield Park is a fine Elizabethan mansion.

Population 2909

Outdoor Leisure

FISHING

Coarse Fishing
Fishing on the River Ouse. For
information and permits contact the
National Rivers Authority.
☎ 0323 762691

Ardingly College Pond
Contact Mr B Windsor.
☎ 0444 455749

Ardingly Reservoir
☎ 0444 892549

Special Interests

GARDENS

Borde Hill Garden
Near Balcombe
Over 40 acres of gardens with rare trees
and plants. Playground, restaurant,
conference facilities.

Leigh Manor
Ansty
5 acres of gardens, laid out with the help
of Gertrude Jekyll.
☎ 0444 413428

Dartford

Wat Tyler's mob attacked and killed a Poll Tax collector here in 1381, so starting the infamous Peasants' Revolt. By the 16th century labour relations were smoother and allowed the establishment of England's earliest paper mill. Modern Dartford has a bustling town centre with Central Park (famous for floral displays) at its heart, a children's playground and the annual Dartford Show.

Market day Thursday
Early closing Wednesday
Population 63,064

Outdoor Leisure

FISHING

Coarse Fishing
Fishing on the Darent. For information and permits contact the National Rivers Authority.
☎ 0732 838858
☎ 0323 762691
☎ 0734 535000

GOLF

Bexley Heath Golf Club
Mount Road, Bexley Heath
Set in hilly parkland; visitors welcome during the week and at weekends with a member.
☎ 081 303 4232

Dartford Golf Club Ltd
The Clubhouse, Dartford Heath
Visitors with membership of another club are welcome on weekdays by reservation and at weekends with a member only.
☎ 0322 226409

HORSE RIDING

Eaglesfield Equestrian Centre
West Yoke, Ash
Riding instruction, schooling, dressage, varied hack and livery.
☎ 0474 873925/872242

WALKING AND RAMBLING

Darent Valley Path
5-mile path follows the River Darent, starts at the park behind the public library.

Dartford Heath
West of town centre
40 acres of informal open heathland.

Special Interests

ARTS AND CRAFTS

David Evans and Company
Bourne Road, Crayford
Silk production, handprinting and finishing. Craft shop. Coffee shop.
☎ 0322 559401

FARM PARKS

Stone Lodge Farm Park
106 London Road, Stone
Working farm park and museum. Rare breeds, demonstrations and wagon rides. Tea room.
☎ 0322 343456

GARDENS

St John's Jerusalem Garden
Off the A225 at Sutton-at-Hone
A large garden with the River Darent forming a moat around a 13th century chapel, now converted to a billiard room.

GUIDED TOURS

Domesday Churches Trail
Full and half day guided excursions brings together eleven churches in Dartford and the surrounding villages.
☎ 0322 343243

HISTORIC BUILDINGS

St Margarets Church
South of Dartford at Darenth
One of the oldest churches in Britain built partly of brick and tile from the nearby Roman Villa.
☎ 0322 227153 for viewing

97

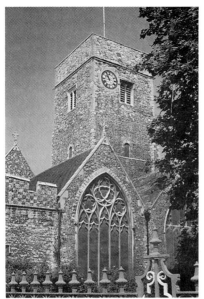
Dartford Parish Church

Dartford Borough Museum
Market Street
Programme of exhibitions on local
history, geological and natural history.
Reconstructed drapers shop.
☎ 0322 343555

NATURAL HISTORY

Joydens Wood
320-acre mixed woodland. Woodland
Trust.

RAILWAYS

North Downs Steam Railway
Stone Lodge
Railway overlooking the River Thames.
☎ 0322 228260

THEATRES

Orchard Theatre
Home Gardens
☎ 0322 343333

Wat Tyler Public House
Half-timbered pub where Tyler and his
men are reputed to have stopped for a
drink on their way to London during the
rebellion of 1381.

Water Sports

SWIMMING

FantaSeas
Off the M25 near Dartford
Indoor water park; slides, flumes,
whirlpools and spas.
☎ 0322 288811

Wat Tyler Public House

HISTORIC HOUSES

St John's Jerusalem
Off the A225 at Sutton-at-Hone
National Trust property with large
moated garden.

FantaSeas

One of the original Cinque ports, Deal is now a peaceful seaside resort and fishing centre. Although treacherous to shipping, the Goodwin Sands shelter the harbour and provide a safe anchorage for large and small vessels. Deal Castle, one of three fortresses built by Henry VIII within four miles of one another, was constructed in the shape of a six-petalled flower.

The small town, with its old-fashioned cottages packed tightly together, makes a charming place for a holiday. It has a shingle beach where fishing boats are still drawn up and the promenade and 1000 foot long pier are places for pleasant walks.

i Town Hall
High Street
☎ 0304 369576

Market day Saturday
Early closing Thursday
Population 26,548

Multi-Activity Holidays

MULTI-ACTIVITY CENTRES

East Kent Field Centre
Beaconhill Cottage, Great Mongeham
Walking, botany, painting, history and
natural history courses.
☎ 0304 372809

Outdoor Leisure

CAMPING AND CARAVANNING

Leisuresope Deal
Golf Road
30 pitches for touring caravans; 5 static
caravans for hire.
☎ 0304 363332

FISHING

Sea Fishing
Contact the Tourist Information Centre.
☎ 0304 369576

GOLF

Walmer and Kingsdown Golf Club ♦18
The Leas, Kingsdown
Cliff top setting, members of another
club welcomed.
☎ 0304 373256

Special Interests

FESTIVALS AND FAIRS

August
Music Festival. Contact the Tourist
Information Centre for details.

GARDENS

Northbourne Court Garden
Home Farm, Betteshanger
Tudor terraced garden.
☎ 0304 611281

99

GUIDED TOURS

Town Trail
Contact the Tourist Information Centre
for details.
☎ 0304 369576

HERITAGE

Sandown Castle
North end of seafront
Another of Henry VIII's coastal forts,
now mainly destroyed by the sea.

HISTORIC BUILDINGS

Deal Castle
Victoria Road
Built in 1540 as the largest of Henry
VIII's coastal defences. Museum,
exhibitions and pictures. Sound Alive
personal stereo tours available.
☎ 0304 372762

MUSEUMS

Costume and Accessories Museum
18 Gladstone Road
☎ 0304 361971

Deal Archaeological Collection
Deal Library, Broad Street
Finds covering 5000 years.
☎ 0304 374726

Maritime and Local History Museum
St Georges Road
Boats, models and other maritime
exhibits.
☎ 0304 362837

Time-Ball Tower
Victoria Parade
Satellite communications, signalling
and time.
☎ 0304 360897

Victoriana Museum
Town Hall

PIERS AND PROMENADES

Deal Pier
Pleasant walks along the promenade and
the 1000-foot-long pier.

Water Sports

SWIMMING

Tides Leisure Pool
Victoria Park
☎ 0304 373399

YACHTING

Dover Sea School
Moving to Ramsgate 1991
Day cruising and courses for two days
and over in Channel, North Sea,
Thames Estuary and Continental
waters.
☎ 0843 852858

Tides Leisure Pool

Dorking is surrounded by some of the finest scenery in Surrey. The High Street follows the route of the Roman Stone Street which once intersected the ancient Pilgrim's Way. Dickens stayed at the White Horse Inn, parts of which date back to the 15th century. The Burford Bridge Hotel, known as the Hare and Hounds in the 19th century, is where Lord Nelson finally separated from Lady Nelson. Twelve counties can be seen from the top of the tower on Leith Hill.

Market day Friday
Early closing Wednesday
Population 14,830

Indoor Sports

SQUASH

Dorking Lawn Tennis and Squash Club
Ridgeway Road
☎ 0306 889668

Dorking Town Squash Club
Reigate Road
☎ 0306 886118

Friends Provident Squash Club
Pixham Lane
☎ 0306 889020

Multi-Activity Holidays

SPECIAL INTEREST CENTRES

Coomb Farmhouse Countryside Training Centre
Balchins Lane, Westcott
An excellent range of wildlife habitats to study.
☎ 0306 885080

Outdoor Leisure

CAMPING AND CARAVANNING

Camping and Caravanning Club Site
Polesden Lacey
128 pitches.
☎ 0372 56844 before 8pm

FISHING

Coarse Fishing
Fishing on the Thames. For information and permits contact the National Rivers Authority.
☎ 0732 838858
☎ 0323 762691
☎ 0734 535000

Old Bury Hill Lake
☎ 0306 883621

GOLF

Betchworth Park Golf Club (Dorking) Ltd ⛳
Reigate Road
Visitors welcome with reservation, handicap certificate required.
☎ 0306 882052

Dorking Golf Club ⛳
Chart Park
Visitors welcome on weekdays without reservation.
☎ 0306 886917

HORSE RIDING

Dorking Riding School
Downs Meadow, Ranmore Road
Mainly weekly riders standing bookings, general purpose hacks on North Downs, woodland and farmland.
☎ 0306 881718/882127

Parkhurst Horse Training Facilities
Lodgelands, Bognor Road, Beare Green
Reschooling for problem horses, holiday courses, livery, schooling and general purpose instruction.
☎ 0306 711869

Partridge Stables
Partridge Lane, Newdigate
General instruction, career and competition training.
☎ 0306 77307

TENNIS

Dorking Lawn Tennis and Squash Club
☎ 0306 889668

WALKING AND RAMBLING

Box Hill
There are pleasant walks around Box Hill and also at Ranmore Common, Leith Hill and Brockham Green.

Special Interests

ART GALLERIES

Gomshall Mill & Gallery
Off the A25 at Gomshall
Gallery, antiques, craft shops and
restaurant.
☎ 048641 2433

Westcott Gallery
4 Guildford Road, Westcott
Contemporary Surrey artists.
☎ 0306 76261

ARTS AND CRAFTS

The Hannah Peschar Gallery
Standon Lane, Ockley
Art centre and country garden.
☎ 0306 79269

COUNTRY PARKS

Box Hill
1 mile north of Dorking on the A24
Country park on the edge of the North
Downs. Nature trails and walks through
woods and chalk downland.
☎ 0306 885502

FARM PARKS

Chapel Farm Animal Trail
Chapel Farm, Westhumble
Day to day life on a working 200-acre
livestock farm.
☎ 0306 882865

FESTIVALS AND FAIRS

June
Box Hill Music Festival. Contact the
Tourist Information Centre for details.

GARDENS

Polesden Lacey
Great Bookham
Rose garden and almost 1600 acres of
gardens, avenues, woodland and walks.
☎ 0372 452048/458203

HISTORIC BUILDINGS

Leith Hill Tower
18th century tower on the highest point
in south-east England.

Polesden Lacey
Great Bookham
Regency villa, remodelled after 1906.
Collections of furniture, paintings,
porcelain and tapestries. Extensive
grounds.
☎ 0372 58203/52048

NATURAL HISTORY

Box Hill
590 feet. Named after the box trees
which grow on it. Other trees, wildlife
and natural features.

The Sheepleas
Off the A246 near East Horsley
271 acres of beautiful beechwoods, open
grassland and wild flowers.

THEATRES

Dorking Halls
☎ 0306 885001

Water Sports

SWIMMING

Dorking Swimming Centre
Reigate Road
☎ 0306 887722

Polsden Lacey

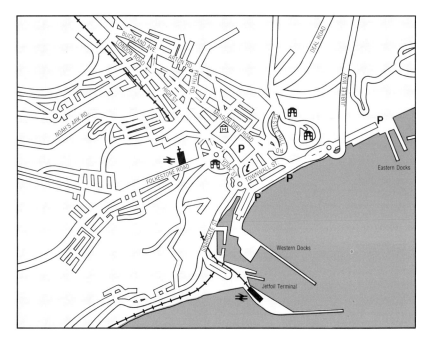

Famous for its chalky white cliffs and principal of the ancient Cinque ports, Dover is even more renowned as a busy cross-channel ferry terminus. As the traditional gateway to England from continental Europe, Dover has been at the focus of numerous expeditions, attacks and invasions over the years and is therefore steeped in history.

i   Townwall Street
☎ 0304 205108

Market days Tuesday, Thursday, Saturday
Early closing Wednesday
Population 34,304

Aerial Sports

GLIDING

Channel Gliding Club
Waldershare Park
☎ 0304 824888

Indoor Sports

LEISURE CENTRES

Dover Leisure Centre
Townwall Street
☎ 0304 201145

Outdoor Leisure

CAMPING AND CARAVANNING

Hawthorn Farm
Martin Mill
250 pitches for tents, touring and motor caravans.
☎ 0304 852658

FISHING

Sea Fishing
Contact the Tourist Information Centre.
☎ 0304 205108

WALKING AND RAMBLING

North Downs Way
From Gravesend to Dover, part of its route follows the ancient Pilgrim's Way. Follow the acorn symbol.

103

Special Interests

GARDENS

Goodnestone Park
Off the B2046
Woodland and walled garden areas; trees, shrubs and roses; connections with Jane Austen.
☎ 0304 840218

The Pines Garden
St Margarets at Cliffe
Garden features large lake and waterfall.
☎ 0304 852764

HERITAGE

Grand Shaft
Snargate Street
140-foot Napoleonic spiral staircase cut into the white cliffs.
☎ 0304 201066

The Pharos
This Roman lighthouse has stood next to the Castle for nearly 2000 years and is the tallest surviving Roman structure in Britain.

HISTORIC BUILDINGS

Crabble Corn Mill
Lower Road, River
Watermill built in 1812, recently restored to full working order.
☎ 0304 823292

Dover Castle
First fortified in prehistoric times and an important military installation up to the Second World War. Exhibition of military history.
☎ 0304 201628

The Roman Painted House
New Street
Roman town house with wall paintings, Roman central heating and history displays.
☎ 0304 203279

St Edmund's Chapel
Built in 1253, dissolved in 1544 and put to a variety of uses before being reconsecrated in 1968.

St Mary-in-Castro Church
Saxon church in the Castle grounds.

MUSEUMS

The Bay Museum
St Margarets at Cliffe
Martime, wartime and local history.
☎ 0304 852764

Dover Museum
Local and social history.
☎ 0304 201066

Dover Transport Museum
Connaught Pumping Station
Local transport history.
☎ 0304 204612

Maison Dieu
Biggin Street
Built 1203 and now part of the Town Hall. Magnificent interior contains items related to the Cinque Ports.
☎ 0304 201200

Old Town Gaol
Biggin Street
Full reconstruction of Victorian prison life and a murder trial.
☎ 0304 242766

The White Cliffs Experience
Market Square
Spectacular new development which incorporates Dover Museum and The Historium, a hi-tech audio-visual treatment of the town from the Roman invasion to WWII. Also the Time and Tide Theatre, a bistro and shops.
☎ 0304 214566

Old Town Gaol Museum

WILDLIFE PARKS

The Butterfly Centre
Swingfield
Butterflies and wildlife.
☎ 0303 83244

Water Sports

YACHTING

Kent Sailing School
45 Castle Street
Courses on modern yacht, short sea crossings and longer passages.

The nuclear power station which dominates the area also guarantees isolation. The national nature and bird reserve covers 12,000 acres.

Outdoor Leisure

BIRDWATCHING

Boulderwall
RSPB bird sanctuary.

FISHING

Sea Fishing
The steep shingle banks are a popular spot for anglers.

Special Interests

HISTORIC BUILDINGS

Dungeness Lighthouse
Recently restored and now open to the public, the lighthouse operated until 1961 when the atomic power station obscured its light.

Dymchurch is an old smuggling port with good sandy beaches and a light railway running across Romney Marsh – a land of mists and mysteries.

Outdoor Leisure

CAMPING AND CARAVANNING

Dymchurch Caravan Park
St Mary's Road
☎ 0303 872303

E & J Piper Caravan Park
St Mary's Road
20 pitches for touring and motor caravans.
☎ 0303 872103

WALKING AND RAMBLING

Romney Marsh Walks
Six circular walks around the Romney Marshes. Contact Shepway District Council for details.
☎ 0303 850388

Fishing boats at Dymchurch

Special Interests

FESTIVALS AND FAIRS

Dr Syn Carnival
Every other summer Russel Thorndike's story of Dr Syn, a fictional vicar of Dymchurch whose alter-ego was a smuggler, is reenacted on the beach.

FUN PARKS

Feathers
Sea front amusement park.

MUSEUMS

Martello Tower 24
One of a chain of 74 built to repel Napoleon, now houses a historical display.
☎ 0303 873684

RAILWAYS

Romney, Hythe and Dymchurch Railway
14 miles of 15-inch gauge railway across Romney Marsh.
☎ 0679 62353

105

A good sunshine, temperature and rainfall record make Eastbourne a popular seaside resort. High white cliffs to the south-west ensure that its shingle beach is well sheltered from the sea winds. Established as a resort in 1780, when four of George III's children spent their summer holidays here, Eastbourne has continued to flourish ever since. Today it supplements all the attractions of a traditional seaside resort – formal gardens, promenade and pier – with the widest possible range of amusements and activities.

i Cornfield Road
☎ 0323 411400

i ✳ Eastbourne Pier
Marine Parade
☎ 0323 411800

Early closing Wednesday

Indoor Sports

LEISURE CENTRES

Cavendish Sports Centre
Eldon Road
☎ 0323 647683

Hampden Park Sports Centre
Brodrick Road
☎ 0323 509859

Sundowners Leisure Centre
Pevensey Bay Road
☎ 0323 762459

SQUASH

Hampden Park Sports Centre
☎ 0323 509859

Sundowners Leisure Centre
☎ 0323 762459

Outdoor Leisure

CYCLING

South Down Cycles
10-12 South Street
☎ 0323 30795

FISHING

Coarse Fishing

Arlington Reservoir
Telephone the fishing lodge for details.
☎ 0323 870810

Compleat Angler Tackle Shop
Day tickets available.
☎ 0323 24740

Tony's Tackle Shop
211 Seaside
☎ 0323 31388

Sea Fishing

Eastbourne Angling Association
☎ 0323 23442

Nomads Angling Club
☎ 0323 20836

The Pier
Night fishing by arrangement with night watchman.
☎ 0323 410466 Management Office

GOLF

Downs Golf Club 🏌
East Dean Road
Visitors welcome all week and after
1 pm on Sundays.
☎ 0323 21844/20827 Secretary

Royal Eastbourne Golf Club 🏌
Paradise Drive
Visitors with a handicap certificate welcome. Cottage accommodation available.
☎ 0323 30412/29738 Secretary

Willingdon Golf Club 🏌
Southdown Road
Visitors welcome, telephone beforehand.
☎ 0323 410983/410981 Secretary

TENNIS

The Ball Park
Rosebery Avenue
☎ 0323 509802

Cavendish Sports Centre
☎ 0323 64783

WALKING AND RAMBLING

The Weald Way
80-mile path from Gravesend to Eastbourne through Weald and downland scenery.

Special Interests

ANTIQUES

Douglas Barnsley
46 Cornfield Road
☎ 0323 33666

AQUARIUMS

Redoubt Fortress Aquarium
Royal Parade
Walk-through underground aquarium; tropical, marine and freshwater fish.
☎ 0323 410300

ART GALLERIES

Towner Art Gallery and Local History Museum
Manor Gardens, High Street
Large collection of 19th and 20th century paintings and prints and work from local artists. Exhibition programme.
☎ 0323 411688

FARM PARKS

Seven Sisters Sheep Centre
Birling Manor Farm, East Dean
Lambing, shearing and milking, spinning displays. Sheep milk products for sale.
☎ 0323 423302

FESTIVALS AND FAIRS

May
Folk Festival

June
Women's International Tennis Tournament

FOOD AND DRINK

Seven Sisters Sheep Centre
☎ 0323 423302

GARDENS

Motcombe Park
Gardens and lake. Source of the Bourne stream which gives Eastbourne its name.

MUSEUMS

Eastbourne Heritage Centre
Carlisle Road
Local history.
☎ 0323 411189

How We Lived Then Museum
20 Cornfield Terrace
A century of social history; over 35,000 exhibits in authentic old shops.
☎ 0323 37143

Lifeboat Museum
King Edwards Parade
RNLI history and displays.

The Redoubt Fortress
Royal Parade
Restored Napoleonic fortress with regimental displays, local and maritime history and an aquarium.
☎ 0323 410300

Eastbourne Pier

Tower 73
King Edward's Parade
Number 73 in the chain of Martello towers built to repel Napoleon.
Military history.
☎ 0323 410440

Towner Art Gallery and Local History Museum
The history of Eastbourne to the Edwardian era.
☎ 0323 411688

ORNAMENTAL PARKS

Carpet Gardens
Floral displays lining the seafront.

Devonshire Park
Town centre

Gildredge Park
Setting for an art gallery and museum.

Hampden Park
Lake and woods; sports facilities.

Helen Gardens
Western Promenade

Princes Park
Royal Parade
With boating lake and miniature golf.

PIERS AND PROMENADES

Eastbourne Pier
Opened 1872 and beautifully preserved.
Amusements, discos, live entertainment.
☎ 0323 410466

Eastbourne Promenade
Three-tier promenade, flower gardens, sports activities, Dotto trains.

THEATRES

Congress Theatre
Carlisle Road

Devonshire Park Theatre
Compton Street

Royal Hippodrome
Seaside Road

Winter Garden Theatre
Compton Street

THEME PARKS

Fort Fun
Royal Parade
All the excitement of the Wild West and other amusements.
☎ 0323 645522

Treasure Island
Royal Parade
Life-size wild animal models, galleon, rigging and other amusements.
☎ 0323 411077

WILDLIFE PARKS

The Butterfly Centre
Royal Parade
☎ 0323 645522

Water Sports

BOAT HIRE

Bluebird Speedboats
Pier Head
☎ 0323 765559

BOAT TRIPS

Allchorn Brothers
Operate from the beach between the pier and bandstand.
☎ 0323 34701

Bluebird Speedboats
☎ 0323 765559

CANOEING

Cuckmere Valley Canoe Club
Contact I J Paterson, 63 Pashley Road.

SWIMMING

Motcombe Swimming Pool
Motcombe Road
☎ 0323 410748

Sovereign Centre
Royal Parade
33-metre gala pool, wave pool, diving pools and flume.
☎ 0323 412444

With a charter dating from 1221, East Grinstead has developed around a compact Sussex market town. The High Street is flanked by largely 16th century timber-framed houses and a large parish church, rebuilt to James Wyatt's designs at the end of the 18th century. Sackville College is in fact a set of Jacobean almshouses built round an elegant courtyard. It was founded as a home for the poor and disabled by the Earl of Dorset in 1609, and is built in sandstone.

A maze of roads run southwards from East Grinstead into the heath and woodland of Ashdown Forest. There are plenty of stopping places and picnic spots.

Market day Saturday
Early closing Wednesday
Population 22,394

Adventure Sports

SHOOTING

Horne Clay Pigeon Club
☎ 034 284 2986

Indoor Sports

LEISURE CENTRES

Kings Centre
Moat Road
Sports hall, solarium, bar.
☎ 0342 328616

SQUASH

Kings Centre
☎ 0342 328616

Outdoor Leisure

BIRDWATCHING

Good birdwatching at Spring Hill Wildfowl Park and Weir Wood Reservoir.

FISHING

Coarse Fishing

Fen Place Mill
☎ 0342 715466

Scarletts Lake
☎ 0342 850414

Weir Wood Reservoir
Forest Row
☎ 034 282 2731

GOLF

Ashdown Forest Hotel and Golf Course ⚑
Chapel Lane, Forest Row
Golf breaks catered for. Visitors welcome; telephone first.
☎ 0342 82 48666

Holtye Golf Club ⚑
Holtye Common, Cowden
Undulating forest course with large practice ground.
☎ 0342 850635

Royal Ashdown Forest Golf Club (Old Course) ⚑
Forest Row
Visitors welcome, advisable to telephone beforehand.
☎ 034 282 2018/3014

Royal Ashdown Forest (New Course) ⚑
Forest Row
☎ 034 282 4866

HORSE RIDING

Belmoredean Stud and Livery Stables
Little Champions Farm, Maplehurst Road, West Grinstead
Facility centre and livery service.
☎ 0403 864635

WALKING AND RAMBLING

Worth Way
6-mile walk to Crawley along a disused railway line.
☎ 0444 458166

Special Interests

GARDENS

Standen
Interesting $10^{1}/_{2}$ -acre garden.
☎ 0342 323029

109

HISTORIC BUILDINGS

High Street
Conservation area; varying styles from 14th century timber-framed to Georgian and Regency buildings.

Old Place
On the B2028 at Lindfield
Timber-framed 1590 house restored by stained glass artist Charles Eames Kempe.

Sackville College
Early Jacobean almshouse with original furniture.

St Augustine's Church
Scaynes Hill
Large oak crucifix stands in the churchyard.

HISTORIC HOUSES

Hammerwood House
3¹/₂ miles east of East Grinstead
1792 house the work of Benjamin Latrobe, architect of the White House and the Capitol in Washington. Costume collection, camera collection; guided tours.
☎ 0342 850594

Priest House
South at West Hoathly
15th century timber-framed house with traditional gardens and museum.
☎ 0342 810479

Standen
1¹/₂ miles south of East Grinstead
Designed by Philip Webb and built in 1894, with original wallpaper, textiles, furniture, pictures, electric fittings, conservatory and billiard room.
☎ 0342 323029

MUSEUMS

Priest House Museum
☎ 0342 810479

Town Museum
East Court, College Lane
Local history.
☎ 0342 322511

WILDLIFE PARKS

Spring Hill Wildfowl Park
Forest Row
Nearly 1000 birds including rare species, in a lovely 10-acre setting.

Water Sports

SWIMMING

Kings Centre
Main pool and teaching pool.
☎ 0342 328616

KENT / Edenbridge / KENT

Several old houses can still be seen in the town's main street, and the church carries a massive 13th century tower crowned by a spire of later date. Impressive gardens can be seen at Hever Castle and a working water mill is open to visitors at Haxted.

Outdoor Leisure

FISHING

Coarse Fishing
Fishing in the Medway. For information and permits contact the National Rivers Authority at Tonbridge.
☎ 0732 838858

Chiddingstone Castle
☎ 0892 870347

GOLF

Edenbridge Golf and Country Club
Crouch House Road
Visitors are unrestricted; driving range.
☎ 0732 865202

Special Interests

FOOD AND DRINK

Chiddingstone Vineyards Ltd
Vexour Farm, Chiddingstone
Winery and 28 acres of vines.
☎ 0892 870277

Hever Castle

GARDENS

Hever Castle Gardens
Italian gardens, lake, colonnades, topiary, maze and rhododendron walk.
☎ 0732 865224

HISTORIC BUILDINGS

Chiddingstone Castle
Gothic-style castle on the edge of a Tudor village. Furnishings and objets d'art from around the world.
☎ 0892 870347

Haxted Watermill and Museum
East of Edenbridge at Haxted
Circa 1850 working mill on the River Eden with two waterwheels. Exhibits and picture gallery.
☎ 0732 865720

Hever Castle
West of Edenbridge at Hever
13th to 15th century moated castle, childhood home of Anne Boleyn. Fine interiors and very attractive grounds; museum.
☎ 0732 865224

MUSEUMS

Haxted Watermill and Museum
East of Edenbridge at Haxted
☎ 0732 865720

Hever Castle
New exhibition depicts the life and times of Anne Boleyn.
☎ 0732 865224

A 20th century memorial commemorates the signing of the Magna Carta by King John in 1215 at Runnymede meadows near Egham. The impressive Royal Holloway College built in 1887 was modelled on a French chateau.

Population 23,000

Indoor Sports

LEISURE CENTRES

Spelthorne Leisure Centre
Knowle Green, Staines
☎ 0784 453171

Special Interests

HERITAGE

Runnymede
Meadow of historical importance: the Magna Carta was signed here in 1215, laying the foundations for a parliamentary constitution in England.

MUSEUMS

Egham Museum
Literary Institute, High Street
Local history.
☎ 0344 843047

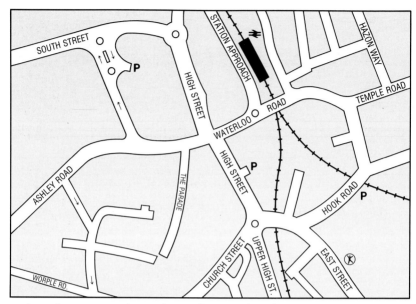

In the 16th century Epsom was famous for its medicinal springs or 'salts'. Nowadays it is better known for its racecourse. The Derby marks the end of the racing season in May and June, and has done since 1780. Racehorses exercise early in the morning and there are some 18th century houses to be seen in Church Street.

Market days Friday, Saturday
Early closing Wednesday

Indoor Sports

LEISURE CENTRES

Rainbow Centre
East Street
Gym, solarium, turkish bath,
swimming pool.
☎ 0372 722283

Ruxley Sports Centre
Ewell High School, Ruxley Lane, Ewell
☎ 0372 744914

Outdoor Leisure

GOLF

Epsom Golf Club 🏌
Longdown Lane South
Visitors welcome; after 12 noon on
Tuesdays and weekends.
☎ 0372 723363

Horton Park Country Club 🏌
Hook Road, Ewell
Driving range.
☎ 081 393 8400

RAC Country Club 🏌
Wilmermatch Lane, Woodcote Park
Two courses. Visitors welcome with
members.
☎ 0372 276311

Surbiton Golf Club 🏌
Woodstock Lane, Chessington
Covered floodlit driving range. Visitors
welcome, book for weekend mornings.
☎ 081 398 3101

HORSE RACING

Epsom Racecourse
Derby Day is in June.
☎ 0372 463072

HORSE RIDING

**Headley Grove Riding and Livery Stables
Ltd**
Headley Common Road, Headley
☎ 0372 376172.

112

WALKING AND RAMBLING

Horton Country Park
North-east of Epsom off the A243
Hard surface footpaths through
woodland and meadow.
☎ 0372 462111

Special Interests

ARTS AND CRAFTS

Horton Park Farm
Spinning and weaving angora wool.
☎ 0372 743984

COUNTRY PARKS

Horton Country Park
North-east of Epsom off the A243
400-acre park features walks, golf and
horse riding. Picnic area; barbecues for
hire.

FARM PARKS

Horton Park Farm
Horton Lane
Rare breeds and unusual animals
including angora goats and rabbits.
Lambing, shearing, spinning and
weaving.
☎ 0372 743984

FESTIVALS AND FAIRS

June
Derby Day at Epsom Racecourse.

THEATRES

Adrian Mann Theatre
North East Surrey College of
Technology, Ewell
☎ 081 393 6660

Bourne Hall
Spring Street, Ewell
Professional and local concerts, drama
and children's events.
☎ 081 393 9571

Epsom Playhouse
Ashley Avenue
☎ 0372 742555

THEME PARKS

Chessington World of Adventures
Leatherhead Road, Chessington
A variety of attractions for children
including Calamity Canyon, the
Smugglers' Galleon, the Fifth
Dimension, a Safari Skyway and of
course, Chessington Zoo.
☎ 0372 727227

Chessington World of Adventures

Circus World

ZOOS

Chessington Zoo
Chessington World of Adventures
☎ 0372 727227

Water Sports

SWIMMING

Rainbow Centre
☎ 0372 726252

113

Esher, a pleasant little town surrounded by open spaces, is the home of Sandown Park Racecourse. Claremont Woods, one mile south of the town, has delightful grounds set out by Capability Brown.

Early closing Wednesday
Population 61,466

Aerial Sports

BALLOONING

Lindsay Muir
Chetwynd, 64 Palace Road, East Molesey
Balloon schooling and instruction.
☎ 081 941 5467

Indoor Sports

SQUASH

Sandown Park Squash Club
More Lane
☎ 0372 467133

Multi-Activity Holidays

SPECIAL INTEREST CENTRES

The Haven Hotel
Portsmouth Road
Discover the Surrey countryside on a Country Wanderer weekend break in the company of a Countryside Service Ranger.
☎ 081 398 0023

Outdoor Leisure

FISHING

Coarse Fishing
Fishing on the Thames. For information and permits contact the National Rivers Authority, Thames Region.
☎ 0734 535000

GOLF

Moore Place Golf Course ⚑
Portsmouth Road
Visitors unrestricted.
☎ 0372 463533

Sandown Park Golf Centre ⚑ ⚑
Sandown Park Racecourse, More Lane
Floodlit 33-bay driving range, visitors unrestricted; public course.
☎ 0372 463340

Surbiton Golf Club ⚑
Woodstock Lane, Chessington
Visitors welcome with prior booking.
☎ 081 398 3101

Thames Ditton and Esher Golf Club ⚑
Marquis of Granby, Portsmouth Road
☎ 081 398 1551

HORSE RACING

Sandown Park Racecourse
1-mile 5 furlong oval course which hosts 27 race days each year. A popular and well organised racecourse.
☎ 0372 463072

HORSE RIDING

South Weylands Equestrian Centre
Esher Road, Hersham
Instruction and residential courses.
☎ 0372 63010/63432

WALKING AND RAMBLING

For details of walks in 1250 acres of woodlands and heathland contact Elmbridge Borough Council.
☎ 0372 462111

Special Interests

GARDENS

Claremont Landscape Garden
Portsmouth Road
England's earliest surviving landscape garden, dating from the early 1700s.
Lake, island, grotto, vistas and glades.
☎ 0372 453401

Winter Sports

SKIING

Sandown Ski School
Sandown Park, More Lane
☎ 0372 465588/467132

114

Farnham has an essentially Georgian character and Castle Street and West Street display excellent examples of architecture of the period. The keep of Farnham Castle was started in 1138 by Henry de Blois, William the Conqueror's grandson. Adjoining this is the 15th to 17th century former residence of the Bishops of Guildford. William Cobbett, author of *Rural Rides*, was born in Farnham and is buried near the porch of the 12th century church. There are pleasant walks in the surrounding North Downs and Weald heathland and rare and unusual species of birds can be seen at Birdworld.

i Farnham Library
Vernon House
28 West Street
☎ 0252 715109

Early closing Wednesday
Population 35,320

Aerial Sports

BALLOONING

Airship Shop Ltd
Abbots Shingle, Botany Hill, Sands
Balloon operators. Balloon souvenirs and accessories. Visitors by appointment only.

Indoor Sports

LEISURE CENTRES

Farnham Sports Centre
Dogflud Way
☎ 0252 723208

SQUASH

Bourne Club
2 Frensham Road
☎ 0252 716144

Farnham Sports Centre
☎ 0252 723208

Multi-Activity Holidays

SPECIAL INTEREST CENTRES

Hogs Back Hotel
Seale
Discover the Surrey countryside on a Country Wanderer weekend break in the company of a Countryside Service Ranger.
0251 82345

Outdoor Leisure

FISHING

Coarse Fishing
Fishing on the Thames. For information and permits contact the National Rivers Authority, Thames Region.
☎ 0734 535000

GOLF

Farnham Park Golf Course
Folly Hill
☎ 0252 715216

Farnham Golf Club Ltd
The Sands
Woodland and parkland course. Visitors with handicap welcome if introduced by a member.
☎ 0251 83163

Hankley Common Golf Club
Tilford Road, Tilford
Visitors welcome with handicap certificate; weekdays, weekends after 2 pm only.
☎ 0251 253145

HORSE RIDING

Old Park Stables
Old Park Lane
General instruction, schooling, hacking on bridleways, common land and country lanes.
☎ 0252 715492/726503

Priory School of Equitation
Millbridge, Frensham
General instruction, hacking, livery, courses and demonstrations, indoor and outdoor shows.
☎ 0251 253697/254161

115

WALKING AND RAMBLING

North Downs Way
Gravesham to Dover
Follows the Pilgrim's Way for some of
its route.

Special Interests

ANTIQUES

Farnham Antiques Centre
27 South Street
☎ 0252 724475

AQUARIUMS

Underwaterworld
3 miles south-west of Farnham on the
A325 at Holt Pound
Aquarium of fish and marine life.
☎ 0420 22668

ARTS AND CRAFTS

Manor Farm Craft Centre
Seale
Watch craftsmen at work on a variety of
crafts.
☎ 0251 83661

ART GALLERIES

New Ashgate Gallery
Wagon Yard
Work of contemporary artists and
craftsmen.
☎ 0252 713208

West Surrey College of Art & Design
The Hart
Exhibitions by artists, designers and
students.
☎ 0252 722441

FOREST PARKS

Alice Holt Forest Visitor Centre
Bucks Horn Oak
Country walks in ancient woodland.
Visitor centre.
☎ 0420 23666

GARDENS

Old Kiln Museum
Arboretum with more than 100
specimens of trees from all over the
world.
☎ 0251 252300

HERITAGE

Farnham Castle Keep
Castle Hill
Castle keep shell with Norman tower
foundations.
☎ 0252 713393

Waverley Abbey
Off the B3001
Ruins of the first Cistercian Abbey in
England, founded in the 12th century.

MUSEUMS

Farnham Museum
Willmer House, 38 West Street
History and archaeology of the town in
18th century house, home of the
William Cobbett Society.
☎ 0252 715094

Old Kiln Museum
Reeds Road, Tilford
Mainly open-air with farm machinery,
wheelwright's shop and working smithy.
☎ 0251 252300

THEATRES

The Redgrave Theatre
☎ 0252 715301

WILDLIFE PARKS

Birdworld
3 miles south of Farnham on the A325 at
Holt Pound.
Rare and unusual species. Extensive
gardens.
☎ 0252 712843

Water Sports

SWIMMING

Farnham Sports Centre
☎ 0252 723208

Old Kiln Museum

YACHTING

Simanda Yachting Services
8 Grovelands, Lower Bourne
Cruising courses on ocean-going yacht
☎ 0252 714919

Positioned on a navigable inlet of the River Swale, this pretty little town was originally a Saxon settlement. In the 13th century the town earned the title of 'Kings Port' because many of the monarch's fighting ships were built there. The town was also noted for the manufacture of gunpowder, for oyster fishing and, in the 18th century, for the smuggling of wines and spirits. Its well preserved streets contain over 400 listed buildings in all.

The Guildhall, Faversham

i Fleur de Lis Heritage Centre
13 Preston Street
☎ 0795 534542

Market days Tuesday, Friday, Saturday
Early closing Thursday
Population 15,985

Outdoor Leisure

BIRDWATCHING

South Swale Nature Reserve
Between Faversham and Seasalter
Brent geese may be seen; pleasant coastal walks.

CAMPING AND CARAVANNING

Painters Farm Camping and Caravan Site
Painters Forstal, Ospringe
25 pitches for tents, 25 pitches for caravans.
☎ 0795 532995

FISHING

Coarse Fishing
Fishing in Oare Pits. For information and permits contact the National Rivers Authority at Tonbridge.
☎ 0732 838858

Faversham Angling Club
Contact Mr A P Baldock, 5 Kennedy Close.

HORSE RIDING

Willow Farm Horse Centre
Hansletts Lane, Ospringe
General instruction, hacking in woodland and on bridleways; livery and schooling.
☎ 0795 533669

WALKING & RAMBLING

Saxon Shore Way
Gravesend to Rye – the route follows the shoreline as it was in Saxon times and is marked in red by a horned helmet symbol.

A Walk Around Faversham
Leaflet available from the Faversham Society, Fleur de Lis, Preston Street.
☎ 0795 534542

Special Interests

FOOD AND DRINK

Shepherd Neame Brewery
Court Street
Guided tours available by appointment.
☎ 0795 532206

GARDENS

Doddington Place Gardens
5 miles south-west of Faversham
10 acres including Edwardian rock garden.
☎ 0795 86385

Mount Ephraim Gardens
Hernhill
7-acre Edwardian garden featuring daffodils and rhododendrons, rose terraces, topiary and a Japanese rock garden.
☎ 0227 751496/750940

HERITAGE

Stone Chapel
Ospringe
Church building which incorporates the remains of a pagan shrine.
☎ 0795 89202

HISTORIC BUILDINGS

Abbey Street
Restored mediaeval street. A number of historic private houses are open to the public for the annual Faversham Open House Scheme. Contact the Tourist Information Centre for details.

Chart Gunpowder Mills
Westbrook Walk
18th century watermills, the only surviving gunpowder mill in England and part of the gunpowder factory which supplied Nelson and Wellington.
☎ 0795 534542

HISTORIC HOUSES

Belmont
4 miles south-west of Faversham
18th century mansion by Samuel Wyatt, Harris family seat since 1801.
☎ 0795 89202

MUSEUMS

Belmont
Clock collection and mementoes of India.
☎ 0795 89202

Chart Gunpowder Mills
☎ 0795 534542

Fleur de Lis Heritage Centre
13 Preston Street
Local history; barber shop and village telephone exchange.
☎ 0795 534542

Maison Dieu Heritage Museum
Ospringe
Norman and Saxon pottery, glass and jewellery.
☎ 0892 548166

NATURAL HISTORY

Perry Wood
Selling
150 acres of woodland with rabbits, squirrels, foxes and badgers.

South Swale Nature Reserve
Wide range of wildfowl including Brent Geese.

THEATRES

Arden Theatre
Central Car Park
☎ 0795 531334

Water Sports

SWIMMING

Faversham Pool
Cross Lane
☎ 0795 532426

The Warren, Folkestone

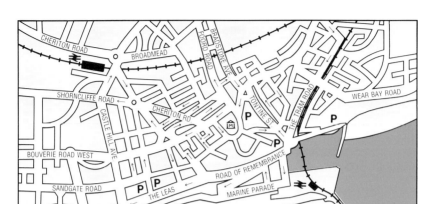

Behind the modern cross-Channel ferry terminus is a quaint old town with cobbled, pub-lined streets. These narrow streets lead down to the wharves where fishing boats still land their daily catches. On a clear day the French coast can be seen from the broad, clifftop walk known locally as The Leas and the sandy beach below is well protected by East Cliff. An interesting lift, powered by water pressure, carries visitors from The Leas to the marine gardens below. Cliff paths run eastwards from Folkestone to Dover across The Warren, a rugged basin with trees, rare flora and interesting fossils.

The Harbour, Folkestone

i Harbour Street
☎ 0303 58594

Market days Thursday, Sunday
Early closing Wednesday, Saturday
Population 44,156

Indoor Sports

LEISURE CENTRES

Folkestone Sports Centre
Radnor Park Avenue
Wide range of facilities including roller dance, steam room and tennis.
☎ 0303 850222

SQUASH

Folkestone Sports Centre
☎ 0303 850222

Mutli-Activity Holidays

MULTI-ACTIVITY CENTRES

Folkestone Activity Holiday Centre
Marine Crescent
☎ 0303 55651

Outdoor Leisure

CAMPING AND CARAVANNING

Black Horse Farm Caravan and Camping Park
358 Canterbury Road, Densole
☎ 0303 892665

Little Switzerland Caravan Park
Wear Bay Road
☎ 0303 52168

The Warren Camping and Caravanning Club Site
The Warren
☎ 0303 55093

CYCLING

Renham's
17 Grace Hill
Cycle hire.
☎ 0303 41884

FISHING

Sea Fishing
Contact the Tourist Information Centre.
☎ 0303 58594

GOLF

Sene Valley, Folkestone and Hythe Golf Club Ltd ⛳
Blackhouse Hill
Downland course overlooking the sea.
Visitors with a handicap welcome.
☎ 0303 268514

HORSE RACING

Folkestone Racecourse
7 miles west of Folkestone at Westenhanger
Flat and national hunt racing at Kent's only racecourse. For information contact Messrs Pratt & Co.
☎ 0444 441111

HORSE RIDING

Limes Farm Training Centre
Limes Farm, Pay Street, Hawkinge
Residential and riding holiday courses, schooling and hacking.
☎ 0303 892335

Saltwood Riding Stables
Hayne Barn, Saltwood
General Instruction.
☎ 0303 260338

TENNIS

Folkestone Sports Centre
Radnor Park Avenue
☎ 0303 850222

WALKING AND RAMBLING

The Warren
Near East Cliff
An area overgrown with trees and wild flowers. Climb to Caesar's Camp for good views.

Special Interests

FESTIVALS AND FAIRS

June
International Folklore Festival

October
Kent Literature Festival – brings together leading writers, poets and broadcasters at the Metropole Arts Centre.

FUN PARKS

Rotunda Amusement Park
☎ 0303 53461

HERITAGE

Sandgate Castle
Castle Road, Sandgate
Built by Henry VIII in 1539 and re-opened to visitors in 1987 after extensive conservation work.
☎ 0303 44032

HISTORIC BUILDINGS

St Mary and Eanswythe Church
The west window commemorates William Harvey, who discovered the circulation of blood.

MUSEUMS

Eurotunnel Exhibition Centre
St Martins Plain, Cheriton High Street
Plans for the Channel Tunnel. Model
railway, maps and viewing tower.
☎ 0303 270111

Folkestone Museum and Art Gallery
Grace Hill
Local, natural and social history and
archaeology.
☎ 0303 850123

Kent Battle of Britain Museum
Hawkinge Airfield
Old fighter base with the country's
largest collection of Battle of Britain
relics.
☎ 0303 893140

PIERS AND PROMENADES

Leas Promenade
Impressive clifftop views across the
English Channel.

THEATRES

Leas Cliff Hall
The Leas
Entertainment centre hosting a variety
of special events.
☎ 0303 54695

Metropole Arts Centre
Host to the Kent Literature Festival.
☎ 0303 44706

WILDLIFE PARKS

The Butterfly Centre
Swingfield
Butterflies from all over the world flying
free in tropical greenhouse gardens.
☎ 0303 83244

Water Sports

SWIMMING

Folkestone Sports Centre
25-metre pool with flume.
☎ 0303 850222

Winter Sports

SKIING

Folkestone Sports Centre
Radnor Park Avenue
Floodlit Dendix slope with tow; caters
for beginners and experienced skiers.
Courses available
☎ 0303 850333

d High Street, Folkestone

Folkestone Activity Holiday Centre

Gillingham is a lively town which caters for a wide range of sporting activities and holds many events throughout the year. Children of all ages will enjoy the Fort Apache adventure playground in the Strand Leisure Park, while those wishing to get away from the crowds will appreciate the local parks, open spaces and woodlands.

i M2 Motorway Services
Farthing Corner
☎ 0634 360323

Market day Monday
Early closing Wednesday
Population 92,929

Indoor Sports

BADMINTON

Medway Badminton Association
Castlemaine Avenue
Five badminton courts and a café/bar lounge are available.
☎ 0634 572187

ICE SKATING

Gillingham Ice Bowl
Gillingham Business Park
Features include disco sessions, hockey matches and individual tuition.
☎ 0634 388477

LEISURE CENTRES

Black Lion Leisure Centre
Mill Road
Facilities include sports and entertainment halls, fitness and health suites, squash courts and pools.
☎ 0634 53784

Centre Sports Priestfield
Gordon Road
Multi-purpose indoor sports arena incorporating cricket, soccer, squash, softball, badminton, tennis, health club, sauna, solarium and a function room.
☎ 0634 281118

The Strand Leisure Park
Off Pier Road
Riverside leisure area; outdoor saltwater pool, pitch & putt, miniature railway, golf, tennis and play park.
☎ 0634 573176/52907/576744

Multi-Activity Holidays

SPECIAL INTEREST CENTRES

Barn Owl Travel
27 Seaview Road
Natural history and birdwatching holidays.
☎ 0634 56759

Outdoor Leisure

BIRDWATCHING

Barn Owl Travel
☎ 0634 56759

Riverside Country Park
Lower Rainham Road
120-acre park with views over the North Kent Marshes and the Medway Estuary
☎ 0634 378987

GOLF

Gillingham Golf Club Ltd 🏌
Woodlands Road
Members of another club with a current handicap are welcome on weekdays.
☎ 0634 55862

WALKING AND RAMBLING

Riverside Country Park
☎ 0634 378987

Saxon Shore Way
From Gravesend to Rye along the coastline of Saxon times. Follow the horned helmet symbol.

Special Interests

COUNTRY PARKS

Riverside Country Park
Lower Rainham Road
A country park of 120 acres suitable for walking, birdwatching and picnicking.
☎ 0634 378987

FESTIVALS AND FAIRS

February
International Showjumping. Contact the Tourist Information Centre for details.

April
Arts Festival

July
Water Festival

HISTORIC BUILDINGS

St Mary Magdalene Church
Norman and Early English architecture.

MUSEUMS

Royal Engineers Museum
Prince Arthur Road
Medals, uniforms, scientific and engineering equipment.
☎ 0634 406397

Urban Heritage Centre
Napier Road
Local history, period classroom.
☎ 0634 570392

NATURAL HISTORY

Berengrave Nature Reserve
Former chalk pit.
☎ 0634 378987

Water Sports

DIVING

South East Diving Centre
140 Richmond Road
☎ 0634 579624

SWIMMING

Splashes Swimming Pool
Bloors Lane, Rainham
A leisure pool featuring a lagoon, flume, wave machine, water cannon, fountains and waterfalls. Fitness and sunbed facilities are also available.
☎ 0634 377509

YACHTING

Gillingham Marina
☎ 0634 54386

Glynde is beautifully situated on the South Downs. Apart from its 18th century Renaissance-style church and the historic Glynde Place, it is also notable as the venue for the world famous Glyndebourne Festival.

Special Interests

FESTIVALS AND FAIRS

May - August
Glyndebourne Festival Opera at Glyndebourne Opera House. Contact the Tourist Information Centre for details.

HISTORIC HOUSES

Glynde Place
The home of Viscount Hampden, a 16th century brick and flint house built around a courtyard. Interesting interior and art collection.
☎ 0273 858337

Godalming was once a staging post on the London to Portsmouth Road, and in 1689, Peter the Great of Russia dined in one of the coaching houses that still exists in the High Street today. An old wool town, its narrow streets have half-timbered inns and houses dating from the 16th to 18th centuries. They surround the eight-sided Old Town Hall which is now used as a museum.

Market day Tuesday, Friday
Early closing Wednesday
Population 18,204

Indoor Sports

LEISURE CENTRES

Godalming Leisure Centre
Broadwater Park, Summers Road
☎ 0483 417282

SQUASH

Guildford and Godalming Rugby Club
Broadwater, Guildford Road
☎ 0483 422514

Multi-Activity Holidays

SPECIAL INTEREST CENTRES

Inn on the Lake
Ockford Road
Discover the Surrey countryside on a Country Wanderer weekend break in the company of a Countryside Service Ranger.
☎ 0306 730851

Outdoor Leisure

CYCLING

Cyclists Touring Club
69 Meadrow
Cycling tours and holidays in Britain and overseas.
☎ 0483 417217

FISHING

Coarse Fishing
Fishing on the Thames. For information and permits contact the National Rivers Authority.
☎ 0734 535000

GOLF

Bramley Golf Club 🏌
On the A281 at Bramley
Visitors welcome Monday to Friday with current handicap certificate.
☎ 0483 893042

Gatton Manor Hotel and Golf Club 🏌
East of Godalming at Ockley
Undulating wooded course with scenic water holes; visitors welcome weekdays and Saturdays until 12 noon.
☎ 0306 79555/6

Shillinglee Park Golf Course 🏌
Off the A283 at Chiddingfold
☎ 0428 653237

West Surrey Golf Club 🏌
Enton Green
Wooded parkland. Visitors welcome, phone prior to visiting.
☎ 0483 421275

HORSE RIDING

Greenways Farm and Stables
Off the A3 at Lower Eashing
Basic instruction in riding and jumping, hacking on common and farmland; livery.
☎ 0486 84741

Special Interests

ARTS AND CRAFTS

Mary Wondrausch
Off the B3000 at Compton
Potter working in 17th century style decorated earthenware.
☎ 0483 414097

Thursley Textile Designs
1 Mousehill Lane, Milford
Shop, gallery and workshop.
☎ 0483 424769

GARDENS

Busbridge Lakes
Hambledon Road
40 acres of parkland, lakes, follies and grotto. Nature trails, ornamental waterfowl.
☎ 0483 421955

Winkworth Arboretum
Hascombe
95 acres of rare shrubs and trees, two lakes, floral displays.
☎ 0372 53401

HISTORIC BUILDINGS

Oakhurst Cottage
South of Godalming at Hambledon
Tiny furnished 16th century cottage.
☎ 0248 684733

Old Town Hall
Situated on an island in the High Street, this 1818 building is built on the site of a pre-mediaeval meeting place and is known by locals as 'the Pepperpot'.

St Peter and St Paul
Interior features remains of 9th century carved Saxon stones. Key available from the Vicarage, opposite.

MUSEUMS

Godalming Museum
109a High Street
Local history since prehistoric times.
☎ 0483 426510

NATURAL HISTORY

Witley Common
Near Milford
Nature trails, interesting flora and fauna.
National Trust.
☎ 0428 683207

Water Sports

BOAT HIRE

Farncombe Boat House
Catteshall Lock
Narrowboats, punts, rowing boats and canoes.
☎ 0483 421306

SWIMMING

Godalming Leisure Centre
☎ 0483 417282

Situated at the top of a hill, Goudhurst commands magnificent views across the river valley and the surrounding Weald hopfields, orchards and forests. The 13th century church is right at the top of the hill and attractive tile-hung and weather-boarded houses cluster around it.

Outdoor Leisure

HORSE RIDING

Bedgebury Riding Centre
☎ 0580 211602

Lynx Park
Colliers Green
☎ 0580 211020

Special Interests

GARDENS

Bedgebury National Pinetum
2¹/₂ miles south of Goudhurst on the B2079
Forestry Commission collection of 150 acres of landscaped gardens with lake and streams. Extensive collection of conifers.
☎ 0580 211044

HISTORIC HOUSES

Finchcocks
Impressive Georgian house and garden set in parkland.
☎ 0580 211702

MUSEUMS

Finchcocks
Collection of keyboard instruments. Special events and courses.
☎ 0580 211702

The Thames estuary narrows at Gravesend to become London's river. It is said to be the busiest waterway in the world and much of the town's activities are focused in the quaint riverside area.

i 10 Parrock Street
☎ 0474 337600

Market day Saturday
Early closing Wednesday
Population 53,638

Indoor Sports

LEISURE CENTRES

Cascades Leisure Centre
Thong Lane
☎ 0474 337471/2

Outdoor Leisure

FISHING

Sea Fishing

National Federation of Sea Anglers
45 St Dunstan's Drive
☎ 0474 569851

Tackle Store
40 Windmill Street
☎ 0474 334802

GOLF

Mid Kent Golf Club
Singlewell Road
Visitors with a handicap certificate welcome on weekdays.
☎ 0474 568035/352387

HORSE RIDING

Tollgate Stables
Monks Buildings, Northumberland Bottom, Wrotham Road
Instruction in riding and jumping, holiday courses, livery and hacking.
☎ 0474 564861
☎ 0634 718521 (evenings)

ORIENTEERING

Shorne Wood Country Park
Signposted from the A2
Permanent course.

TENNIS

Record Tennis Centre
Thong Lane
☎ 0474 324526

WALKING AND RAMBLING

Cobham Walks
Six walks in and around the historic village of Cobham, ranging from 3–5 miles. Leaflet available from the Tourist Information Centre.

Gordon Memorial Walk
3-mile walk around Gravesend. Leaflet available from the Tourist Information Centre.

Gravesham: Dickens Country
An exploration of the places around Gravesend associated with Dickens. Contact the Tourist Information Centre.
☎ 0474 337600

Saxon Shore Way
Follows the coastline as it was in Saxon times, from Gravesend to Rye, via Rochester, Gillingham and Faversham.

The Weald Way
80-mile long distance path from Gravesend to Eastbourne.

Special Interests

COUNTRY PARKS

Shorne Wood
160 acres of heathland and woodland.

126

St Georges Shopping Centre

FESTIVALS AND FAIRS

May
Gravesham Riverside Fair

August
Summer Regatta

GARDENS

Camer Park
46 acres of landscaped gardens.

Cobham Hall
50 acres of grounds landscaped by
Humphry Repton.

HISTORIC BUILDINGS

Cobham College
South-east at Cobham
Recently renovated almshouses
originally founded in 1362 as a college
for priests.

The Leather Bottle Inn
South-east at Cobham
Timber-framed village pub which
Dickens used to visit regularly.

Meopham Windmill
Meopham Green
Early 19th century smock mill.
☎ 0474 813218

Milton Chantry
Fort Gardens
14th century leper hospital chapel which
became an inn in the 17th century.
☎ 0474 321520

New Tavern Fort
Fort Gardens
18th to 20th century fort, overlooking
the Thames, with underground
ammunition store and Second World
War exhibition. Contact the Tourist
Information Centre for details.

The Old Forge
Off the A226 at Chalk
Weatherboarded and tiled building
believed by many to be the original of Joe
Gargery's forge in *Great Expectations*.

St George's Church
Built in 1731. A statue of the American
Princess Pocahontas, who died on a
ship off Gravesend, can be seen in the
churchyard.

St Mary's Church
Higham
A 13th century church with many later
additions set on the edge of the marshes.

HISTORIC HOUSES

Cobham Hall
South-east at Cobham
Interior features by James Watt, Inigo
Jones and the Adams brothers.
☎ 0474 823371

Gads Hill Place
Higham
Once the home of Charles Dickens, now
a private girls school.

Owletts
South-east at Cobham
Built in 1683-4 for Bonham Hayes,
features ornate plasterwork. National
Trust.
☎ 0892 890651

MUSEUMS

Gravesham Museum
High Street
History and development of Gravesend
over the last two centuries
☎ 0474 323159

THEATRES

Woodville Halls
Town centre
Multi-purpose venue.
☎ 0474 337459

Water Sports

SWIMMING

Cascades Leisure Centre
Waves, fountains, waterfall and flumes.
☎ 0474 337471/2

YACHTING

Gravesend Sailing Club
Canal Basin
Contact Mrs Barber, 7 Studley Crescent,
Longfield.

North Kent Yachting Association
☎ 0474 321613

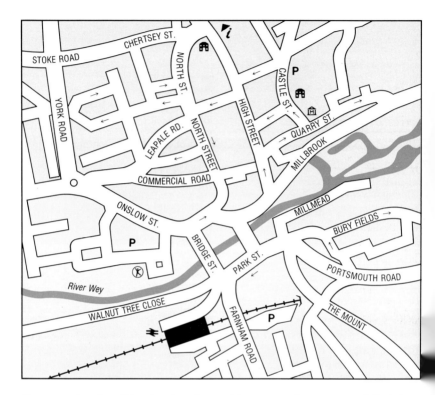

Fine examples of traditional and modern architecture can be seen in Guildford, from the remains of the 12th century castle on Quarry Street to the imposing 20th century cathedral on Stag Hill. Many of the Georgian facades in the High Street conceal much older constructions. The Guildhall is a Tudor building to which a 17th century facade has been added and Abbot's Hospital is a group of 17th century almshouses. Charles Dodgson, better known as Lewis Carroll, the author of *Alice in Wonderland*, is buried in Mount Cemetery. The North Downs narrow to become the spectacular Hog's Back to the west of Guildford.

i The Undercroft
72-74 High Street
☎ 0483 444007

Market days Friday, Saturday
Early closing Wednesday
Population 63,086

Indoor Sports

LEISURE CENTRES

Guildford Sports Centre
Bedford Road
☎ 0483 444777

University of Surrey Sports Hall
Egerton Road
☎ 0483 509201

SQUASH

University of Surrey Sports Hall
☎ 0483 509201

Multi-Activity Holidays

SPECIAL INTEREST CENTRES

Hurtwood Inn
Peaslake
Discover the Surrey countryside on a Country Wanderer weekend break in the company of a Countryside Service Ranger.
☎ 0306 730851

Outdoor Leisure

FISHING

Coarse Fishing
Fishing on the Thames. For information
and permits contact the National Rivers
Authority, Thames Region.
☎ 0734 535000

GOLF

The Drift Golf and Leisure Club ⌐₁₈
The Drift, East Horsley
☎ 04865 4772

Gole Farm Golf Course ⌐₉
Gole Road, Pirbright
☎ 0486 73183

Guildford Golf Club ⌐₁₈
High Path Road, Merrow
Visitors welcome weekdays; with a
member at weekends.
☎ 0483 66765

Puttenham Golf Club ⌐₁₈
Visitors welcome weekdays; weekends
with a member; handicap required.
☎ 0483 810498

Special Interests

ANTIQUES

Guildford Antique Centre
22 Haydon Place
☎ 0483 67817

ART GALLERIES

Guildford House Gallery
155 High Street
Architecturally interesting 17th century
house with wide range of art exhibitions.
☎ 0483 444741

University of Surrey Library Gallery
Stag Hill
Exhibitions usually by contemporary
artists.
☎ 0483 571281 extn 2112

The Watts Gallery
Down Lane, Compton
Memorial gallery containing pictures
and sculptures by G F Watts.
☎ 0483 810235

FARM PARKS

Loseley Park Farm
Loseley Park
Working dairy farm, home of the famous
Loseley dairy products made from Jersey
milk.
☎ 0483 571881

The Old Farm at Shere
Durfold House
Off the A25 at Shere
Farm visit; demonstrations and
exhibitions.
☎ 048641 2976

FESTIVALS AND FAIRS

March
Dicing for Maids' Money

May
County Show

July
Guildford Festival

FOOD AND DRINK

Loseley Dairy Produce
☎ 0483 571881

GARDENS

Clandon Park
West Clandon
Fine garden with parterre, grotto and
Maori House.
☎ 0483 222482

Hatchlands Park
East Clandon
Garden designed by Gertrude Jekyll and
Goodhart-Rendel; currently being
restored.
☎ 0483 222787

GUIDED TOURS

Town Tours
Regular and group tours available.
Contact the Tourist Information Centre
for details.
☎ 0483 444007

HERITAGE

Guildford Castle
Castle Street
Ruined Norman keep. Interesting
grounds with giant chess board.
☎ 0483 444004 Tourism Department

HISTORIC BUILDINGS

Abbotts Hospital
High Street
Founded by George Abbott in 1619 as a
home for the elderly. Fine mediaeval
glass windows and original furnishings.

Guildford Cathedral
Stag Hill
Started in 1936 and consecrated in 1961,
particularly notable for engraved glass,
modern furnishings and embroidery.
☎ 0483 65287

129

The Guildhall
High Street
Restored Tudor building with an ornate 17th century clock projecting yards into the street, and an interesting interior.
☎ 0483 444004 Tourism Department

Holy Trinity Church
The pro-cathedral 1927–1961. Broad unsupported ceiling; fine memorial tomb to the Archbishop George Abbot (1633).

Irvingite Church
North of Albury
Built by a 19th century sect, the Catholic Apostolic Church.

Royal Grammar School
Upper High Street
Founded in 1507.

St Mary's Church
Quarry Street
Largely 17th century; fine interior.

Shalford Mill
On the A281 at Shalford
18th century cornmill with original machinery and waterwheel.
☎ 0372 453401

Watts Mortuary Chapel
Teracotta building designed by the potter Mary Watts. Her husband G F Watts was one of the most popular late Victorian painters. Art nouveau interior.

HISTORIC HOUSES

Albury Park
On the A248 at Albury
Large Victorian country mansion by Pugin.
☎ 048 641 2964

Loseley House
Loseley Park
Elizabethan mansion with decorated ceilings and unusual chalk fireplace. Parklands and farm, famous for Loseley dairy produce.
☎ 0483 571881

MUSEUMS

Guildford Museum
Castle Arch, Quarry Street
Local history, archaeology and Surrey Records Office. Also items concerning Lewis Carroll.
☎ 0483 444750

Hatchlands
☎ 0483 222787

Museum of the Queen's Royal Surrey Regiment
Clandon Park, West Clandon
☎ 0483 222482

Shere Museum
Off the A25 at Shere
Mainly Victorian and later bygones.
☎ 048 641 3245

Womens Royal Army Corps Museum
Queen Elizabeth Park
☎ 0252 24431 extn 8565

ORNAMENTAL PARKS

Stoke Park
Ornamental gardens, paddling pools, sports facilities.

THEATRES

Yvonne Arnaud Theatre
Milbrook
Top quality productions.
☎ 0483 60191

Civic Hall
London Road
Home of the Guildford Philharmonic Orchestra.
☎ 0483 444555

Water Sports

BOAT HIRE

Guildford Boathouse
Millbrook
Boating holidays, narrowboats and cruisers on the rivers Wey and Thames. Tuition available.
☎ 0483 504494

BOAT TRIPS

Guildford Boathouse
Cruises on the River Wey.
☎ 0483 504494

SWIMMING

Guildford Lido
Stoke Park
Outdoor pool open May to September.
☎ 0483 505207

Winter Sports

SKIING

Bishop Reindorp Ski School
Larch Avenue
☎ 0483 504988 (day)/570994 (evenings

Hailsham is a busy market town in a rural setting and the surrounding countryside is well worth exploring. The 15th century church has a splendid tomb of Thomas Lord Dacre, who died in 1533, and his son.

i The Library
Western Road
☎ 0323 840604

Market days Wednesday, Friday
Early closing Thursday
Population 13,600

Outdoor Leisure

FISHING

Coarse Fishing
Fishing on the River Cuckmere. For information and permits contact the National Rivers Authority.
☎ 0732 838858
☎ 0323 762691
☎ 0734 535000

Hailsham Angling Association
Contact Mr A Dean, 5 Garfield Road.

Special Interests

ARTS AND CRAFTS

The Truggery
Coopers Croft, Herstmonceux
Sussex trug baskets made and sold.
☎ 0323 832314

GARDENS

Michelham Priory
Upper Dicker
Tudor barn, working watermill, physic garden and museums in attractive grounds.
☎ 0323 844224

HISTORIC BUILDINGS

Church of St Mary the Virgin
First recorded in 1229 but extensively restored and rebuilt since then; old peal of bells.

Herstmonceux Castle
Off the A271 at Herstmonceux
Built in 1440, one of the earliest brick castles with moat, drawbridge, portcullis and battlements. At present closed, although there is a public footpath which passes by the grounds.

Horselunger Manor
North of Hailsham at Hellingly
16th century manor, restored this century, one of the finest timbered houses in Sussex.

Michelham Priory

Michelham Priory
13th century priory with moat and 14th century gatehouse. Period furniture, musical instruments, tapestries and stained glass.
☎ 0323 844224

MUSEUMS

Heritage Centre
Old Bakery, Market Street
Hailsham Historical and Natural History Society. Seasonal
☎ 0323 840947

Michelham Priory
West of Hailsham at Upper Dicker
13th to 16th century buildings with varied exhibits. Tudor barn, temporary art exhibitions. Working watermill.
☎ 0323 844224

131

In wooded, hilly countryside, Haslemere offers many attractive walks. Harpsichords, lutes and other early musical instruments are made in the town and can be seen at the Dolmetsch Workshop and Museum.

Early closing Wednesday
Population 10,617

Indoor Sports

LEISURE CENTRES

Haslemere Swimming Pool and Squash Courts
Lion Green, Way Hill
☎ 0428 642124

SQUASH

Haslemere Swimming Pool and Squash Courts
☎ 0428 6542124

Outdoor Leisure

BIRDWATCHING

Frensham Country Park
Nightjar and great grey shrike.

FISHING

Coarse Fishing
Fishing available at Great and Little Ponds, day tickets from Farnham Angling Society.

GOLF

Hindhead Golf Club ♘
Churt Road, Hindhead
Heathland, wooded; fairly hilly course. Visitors welcome with a handicap certificate; check prior to visit.
☎ 0428 734614

Shillinglee Park Golf Club ♘
Chiddingfold
Advisable to phone at weekends.
☎ 0428 53237

HORSE RIDING

Circular Horse Ride
A 22-mile horse ride which explores Surrey's countryside, starting from the Devil's Punchbowl at Hindhead. Map available from the library, 91 Wey Hill
☎ 0428 642907

Southern Equitation Livery Centre
Frensham Lane, Wishanger Estate, Churt
All types of livery, private tuition.
☎ 025 125 3461

WALKING AND RAMBLING

Devil's Jumps
Off the A287 at Churt
Three conical hills associated with pagan legend. Stony Jump is owned by the National Trust.

Hindhead, Invalland and Weydown Commons
Just north of Haslemere

Special Interests

ARTS AND CRAFTS

Grayshott Pottery
School Road, Grayshott
Pottery and showroom.
☎ 0428 604404

COUNTRY PARKS

Frensham
Off the A287
Lowland heath which supports all six species of native reptile. The two lakes have safe, sandy beaches. Information Centre.

FESTIVALS AND FAIRS

July
Music Festival

MUSEUMS

Haslemere Educational Museum
High Street
Botany, zoology, geology, history and British birds.
☎ 0428 642112

Water Sports

SWIMMING

Haslemere Swimming Pool and Squash Courts
☎ 0428 642124

132

Hastings Castle was built by William the Conqueror shortly after his invasion in 1066. Ruins survive today, although part of it has been washed away by the sea. In more peaceful times, Hastings became a quiet fishing village and visitors can still admire some 15th to early 19th century houses along the narrow, twisting passages in the old part of the town. John Logie Baird made the world's first television transmission from Queen's Road. Today Hastings is a popular seaside resort with a long shingle beach.

i 4 Robertson Terrace
☎ 0424 718888

✳The Fishmarket
Old Town
☎ 0424 721201

Early closing Wednesday
Population 77,000

Indoor Sports

BADMINTON

Summerfields Sports Centre
Bohemia Road
☎ 0424 722227

ICE SKATING

White Rock Ice Rink
White Rock Road
☎ 0424 425731

LEISURE CENTRES

Summerfields Sports Centre
Multigym, solarium.
☎ 0424 722227

SQUASH

Summerfields Sports Centre
☎ 0424 722227

Outdoor Leisure

FISHING

Coarse Fishing
For information and permits contact the National Rivers Authority at Pevensey Bay.
☎ 0323 762691

Clive Vale Reservoirs
Clive Vale Angling Club
☎ 0424 420370

Sea Fishing
Contact the Tourist Information Centre for details.
☎ 0424 718888

GOLF

Hastings Golf Club ⛳
Battle Road, St Leonards-on-Sea
Visitors are unrestricted.
☎ 0424 852981

HORSE RIDING

Beauport Riding School
Beauport Park, Battle Road
☎ 0424 851424

TENNIS

Alexandra Park
Eight tennis courts.

WALKING AND RAMBLING

Hastings Country Park
Access via East Cliff Railway or by bus to Fairlight
A full events programme featuring Ranger guided walks is available from the Tourist Information Centre.
☎ 0424 718888

St Helens Wood
St Helens Road

Special Interests

ANTIQUES

Maheen Heuduk Antiques
52–54 George Street
☎ 0424 434373

AQUARIUMS

Sea Life Centre
Rock-a-Nore Road
Multi-level viewing of many marine creatures. Café.
☎ 0424 718776

ART GALLERIES

Hastings Museum and Art Gallery
Cambridge Road
Regular exhibitions.
☎ 0424 721202

COUNTRY PARKS

Hastings Country Park
Gorse-covered hills, nature trails.
Contact the Tourist Information Centre
for details.

FACTORY VISITS

Carr Taylor Vineyards
Yew Tree Farm, Westfield
21-acre vineyard with winery,
winemaking machinery and cellars.
☎ 0424 752501

FESTIVALS AND FAIRS

January
Chess Congress

March
Musical Festival

May
Blessing the Sea

October
Hastings Week

FUN PARKS

Jungle Tumble
The Stade, Old Town
Supervised indoor play area.
☎ 0424 425503

Pleasure Island
The Stade, Old Town
Traditional seaside amusements.

GUIDED TOURS

Old Town Walks
Regular guided walks with a member of
the Old Hastings Preservation Society.
Contact the Tourist Information Centre
for details.
☎ 0424 718888

Sightseeing Tour
Open-top bus tours visiting main
attractions, hop on and off as you please.
Contact the Tourist Information Centre
for details.

HERITAGE

Hastings Castle
West Hill
Castle remains with dungeons; 1066
story interpretation centre in siege tent.
☎ 0424 722022

MUSEUMS

Fishermen's Museum
Rock-a-Nore Road
☎ 0424 424787

Hastings Domesday Exhibition
White Rock Theatre
☎ 0424 721210

Hastings Embroidery
Town Hall, Queens Road
74-metre embroidery, made for 900th
anniversary of the Battle of Hastings,
showing great events in British history.
☎ 0424 722022

Hastings Museum and Art Gallery
Local history; geology and zoology;
collections from Asia and Oceania.
☎ 0424 721202

Hastings Museum of Local History
Old Town Hall, High Street
Former town hall with local history,
Norman Conquest and local discovery of
TV by John Logie Baird in 1924.
☎ 0242 721209

Shipwreck Heritage Centre
Rock-a-Nore Road
Sound and light show story of 500-year-
old shipwreck. Treasure exhibition; live
daily pictures of Europe from space.
☎ 0424 437452

ORNAMENTAL PARKS

Alexandra Park
Over 120 acres of flower gardens and
woodland with bowls, tennis, putting
and a boating lake.

White Rock Gardens
Seafront
Park with adventure playground, mini-
golf and a model village.

PIERS AND PROMENADES

Hastings Pier
Arcades and rides and one of the largest
ballrooms on the south coast.

RAILWAYS

East and West Hill Cliff Railways
East Hill Railway runs from Rock-a-
Nore to the Country Park. West Hill
Railway runs from George Street to the
Castle.

THEATRES

Stables Theatre
High Street
☎ 0424 423221

Carr Taylor Vineyards

White Rock Theatre
Variety shows, concerts and plays.
Restaurant.
☎ 0424 722755

THEME PARKS

Smugglers Adventure
St Clements Caves, West Hill
One acre of caves; 50 life-size figures;
lighting and sound effects portraying
smuggling along the coast.
☎ 0424 422964

Haywards Heath grew up around a railway station which neighbouring towns had
refused to accommodate. Its market is the largest in Sussex with regular sales of
livestock, farm machinery, furniture and antiques.

Indoor Sports

LEISURE CENTRES

Dolphin Leisure Centre
Fitness unit, swimming pool, squash
court.
☎ 0444 457337

SQUASH

Dolphin Leisure Centre
☎ 0444 457337

Outdoor Leisure

FISHING

Coarse Fishing
Fishing on the River Ouse. For
information and permits contact the
National Rivers Authority.
☎ 0323 762691

Ditchling Common Pond
3 miles south of Haywards Heath

Special Interests

FARM PARKS

Burstye Soays
Burstye Farm, Lindfield
Farm devoted to a rare breed of sheep,
the Soay.
0444 483376

GARDENS

Borde Hill Garden
North-west at Borde Hill
Garden and parkland. Rare trees and
shrubs and a wide range of floral
displays.
☎ 0444 450326

Wakehurst Place Gardens
Ardingly
Part of the Royal Botanic Gardens. Ponds
and lakes with exotic trees and shrubs.
☎ 0444 892701

HISTORIC BUILDINGS

St Peter's Church
On the B2028 at Ardingly
14th century church features massive
tower; timbered porch; an effigy of a
priest in vestments; five good brasses
and ancient stairs.

St Wilfrids Church
Built in 1863, its old Sussex type of
tower caps the ridge in the centre of
town.

Water Sports

SWIMMING

Dolphin Leisure Centre
Pasture Hill Road
Main pool, diving pool, teaching pool.
☎ 0444 457337

The Heathfield area was once well known for cannon-making. Now you can catch the mood of an old market town by browsing along the Causeway which is tucked behind the busy High Street.

Outdoor Leisure

FISHING

Coarse Fishing
Barrats Park Farm (lower pond). Tickets from Polegate Angling Centre.

GOLF

Horam Park Golf Course ⚑
Chiddingly Road, Horam
Wooded course with several lakes and ponds, floodlit driving range. Visitors welcome, advised to book beforehand.
☎ 043 53 3477

HORSE RIDING

Sky Farm Riding School
Cade Street
General instruction, specialise in children and beginners, livery, hacking and children's courses.
☎ 0435 863132

Special Interests

FACTORY VISITS

Merrydown Cider
Horam Manor
Cider making in a tradition dating from Norman times. Guided tours by appointment.
☎ 043 53 2254

FOOD AND DRINK

Merrydown Cider
Horam Manor
☎ 043 53 2254

St George's Vineyard
Waldron
Vineyard with own label wines. 11th century barn, farm animals and herb garden.
☎ 043 53 2156

MUSEUMS

Sussex Farm Museum
Horam Manor Farm, Horam
Countryside, crafts and old farming methods, nature trail and demonstrations.
☎ 043 53 2597/3161

Herne Bay, on the north coast of Kent, has a seven-mile stretch of shingle beach which attracts visitors throughout the summer months.

i The Bandstand
Central Parade
☎ 0227 361911

Market day Saturday
Early closing Thursday
Population 27,799

Indoor Sports

LEISURE CENTRES

Pier Pavilion
Sports hall, club rooms, roller skating, weights room.
☎ 0227 366921

SQUASH

Pier Pavilion
Two courts.
☎ 0227 366921

Outdoor Leisure

CAMPING AND CARAVANNING

Hillborough Caravan Park
Reculver Road, Hillborough
40 pitches for touring and motor
caravans.
☎ 0227 374618

Westbrook Farm Caravan Park
Sea Street
100 pitches for touring and motor
caravans.
☎ 0227 375586

FISHING

Sea Fishing
Contact the Tourist Information Centre.
☎ 0227 361911

GOLF

Herne Bay Golf Club ⛳
Canterbury Road, Eddington
Visitors with a handicap welcome on
weekdays and weekend afternoons.
☎ 0227 373964

Special Interests

COUNTRY PARKS

Reculver Country Park
3 miles east of Herne Bay on the A299
91-acre country park on an exposed
headland focused around the remains of
a Roman fort; interesting archaeological
site.

Wealden Forest Park
Herne Common
16 acres of English woodland with
indigenous animals. Farmyard,
fishponds.
☎ 0227 712379

HERITAGE

Reculver Towers and Roman Fort
Reculver Country Park
12th century twin towers retained as a
navigation aid when the Saxon church
was demolished in 1809. Remains of 3rd
century Roman fort.
☎ 0227 366444

Herne Windmill

HISTORIC BUILDINGS

Herne Windmill
Kentish smock mill built in 1789,
restored to full working condition with
original machinery.
☎ 0227 361326

MUSEUMS

Herne Bay Museum
The Library, 124 High Street
Local history, archaeology and pictures.
☎ 0227 374896

WILDLIFE PARKS

**Brambles English Wildlife and Rare
Breeds**
Wealden Forest Park, Herne Common
26 acres of English woodland with
indigenous animals. Farmyard,
fishponds.
☎ 0227 712379

Water Sports

YACHTING

Herne Bay Sailing Club Ltd
The Downs
☎ 0227 375650

Herne Bay Yacht Club
Hampton Pier
☎ 0227 369343

Horley is expanding and has been considerably redeveloped but it still retains a 14th century church and a 15th century inn with diamond shaped tile-hanging in the town centre.

Early closing Wednesday

Outdoor Leisure

HORSE RIDING

Burstow Park Riding and Livery Centre
Antlands Lane
General instruction and livery.
☎ 0293 820766

Special Interests

ART GALLERIES

Outwood Art Gallery and Sculpture Park
Green Lane, Outwood
Watercolours, oils, sculpture and crafts, some items for sale.
☎ 0342 842126

HISTORIC BUILDINGS

The Post Mill
Outwood Common
England's oldest working windmill, built in 1665.
☎ 0342 843458

MUSEUMS

The Post Mill
Small agricultural museum; farm animals.
☎ 0342 843458

Water Sports

SWIMMING

Horley Swimming Pool
☎ 0293 784075

A number of fine old houses line The Causeway which leads to an impressive church with a 175-foot shingled spire. Percy Bysshe Shelley was born here at Field Place, in 1792. In 1844 a man sold his watch to buy another man's wife in the Market Square. Horsham provides a good base for walks in St Leonard's Forest – thousands of acres of wooded valleys and heather clad hills.

i Horsham Museum
9 The Causeway
☎ 0403 211661

Early closing Monday, Thursday
Population 38,565

Indoor Sports

LEISURE CENTRES

Broadbridge Heath Sports Centre
Wickhurst Lane, Broadbridge Heath
☎ 0403 211311

Forest Recreation Centre
Comptons Lane
☎ 0403 69619

Park Recreation Centre
Albion Way, Horsham Park
Sports hall, courses and classes. Football tennis and bowls in the park.
☎ 0403 68561

Outdoor Leisure

FISHING

Game Fishing

Wattlehurst Lake
Kingsfold
Trout fishery. Tickets from Mr G Nye
☎ 0306 79341

GOLF

Mannings Heath Golf Club ⓘ
Goldings Lane, Mannings Heath
Undulating wooded course. Visitors
welcome with handicap certificate and
by prior arrangement.
☎ 0403 210168

HORSE RIDING

Naldretts Farm
Off the A281 between Bucks Green and
Billingshurst
☎ 0403 822403

TENNIS

Park Recreation Centre
☎ 0403 68561

Weald Recreation Centre
☎ 0403 784245

Special Interests

ART GALLERIES

Lennards Gallery
Okehurst Road, Billingshurst
Octagonal gallery with paintings,
furniture and designer craft work.
☎ 0403 782692

COUNTRY PARKS

Buchan Country Park
On the A264
160 acres of woodland and glades, two
ponds.

Southwater County Park
Lakes and landscaped area in an old
brickworks.
☎ 0403 731218

GARDENS

Leonardslee Gardens
Lower Beeding
Spring-flowering shrubs, camellias and
specimen trees.
☎ 0403 891212

MUSEUMS

Horsham Museum
9 The Causeway
Displays of local history and rural crafts
in a listed 16th century timber-framed
house.
☎ 0403 54959

Water Sports

SWIMMING

Park Swimming Centre
Hurst Road
☎ 0403 58078

Hove is characterised by its elegant Regency terraces with bow fronts, tall pilasters
and green lawns. Originally a fishing village with smuggling connections, it became
fashionable as a seaside resort after the Prince Regent's patronage of neighbouring
Brighton. Edward VII also enjoyed strolling along Hove's seafront. All Saints' Church
has a richly-carved screen, a high altar and the tomb of Sir George Everest (1790-1866)
after whom the world's tallest mountain is named.

King Alfred Leisure Centre
Kingsway
☎ 0273 746100

Town Hall
Norton Road
☎ 0273 775400

Early closing Wednesday
Population 67,137

Aerial Sports

HANG GLIDING

Free Flight
274 New Church Road
☎ 0273 411239

Sussex College of Hang Gliding
Sussex College
☎ 0273 733914/609925

139

Indoor Sports

LEISURE CENTRES

King Alfred Leisure Centre
Kingsway
Solarium, sauna and two sports halls.
☎ 0273 822011

TENPIN BOWLING

King Alfred Leisure Centre
Kingsway
22-lane bowling alley.
☎ 0273 772828 (Bowling Information)

Outdoor Leisure

CRICKET

Sussex County Cricket Club
County Ground
☎ 0273 732161 (for fixtures)

FISHING

Coarse Fishing
River Arun, west bank from Houghton
Bridge to Timberley Wood and the
River Adur, north bank from Bay Bridge
to Tenchford. Tickets from:
Ken Denman Ltd
2 Marine Place, Worthing

Lagoon Tackle Shop
327 Kingsway, Hove

FOOTBALL

Goldstone Ground
Brighton and Hove Albion home base.
☎ 0273 739535 (match information)

GOLF

West Hove Golf Club ⓑ
369 Old Shoreham Road
Experienced visitors welcome with
reservation.
☎ 0273 413494

TENNIS

Record Tennis Centre
Kingsway
3 tennis courts (open air in summer,
covered in winter)
☎ 0273 206939

Special Interests

ANTIQUES

Angel Antiques
16 Church Road
☎ 0273 562947

ART GALLERIES

Hove Museum and Art Gallery
19 New Church Road
Fine collection of English paintings and
special exhibitions.
☎ 0273 779410

HISTORIC BUILDINGS

West Blatchington Windmill
Holmes Avenue
Unusual hexagonal smock mill dating
from the 19th century, original
machinery. For details contact Hove
Borough Council.
☎ 0273 775400

MUSEUMS

The British Engineerium
Nevill Road
Victorian Goldstone pumping station
with hundreds of steam exhibits.
☎ 0273 559583

Hove Museum and Art Gallery
Museum of art and history; pottery,
porcelain, glass, silver and dolls.
☎ 0273 779410

West Blatchington Windmill
Holmes Avenue
☎ 0273 776017

Water Sports

SWIMMING

King Alfred Leisure Centre
Leisure pools, water slides.
☎ 0273 822011

YACHTING

Marabu Syndicate
55 Hove Park
Cruising area is the Channel and Solent
☎ 0273 501708

A traditional seaside resort attached to a charming old town which is divided by the Royal Military Canal. Dating from Napoleonic times, the Canal is now used for boating.

i Prospect Road Car Park
☎ 0303 267799

Early closing Wednesday
Population 13,700

Outdoor Leisure

CAMPING AND CARAVANNING

Beach Bank Caravan Park
On the A259 between Hythe and Dymchurch
☎ 0303 269484

FISHING

Coarse Fishing
Brockhill Country Park
Day tickets available on site.

Sea Fishing
Contact the Tourist Information Centre.
☎ 0303 267799

GOLF

Hythe Imperial Golf Club
Princes Parade
Flat seaside course with restrictions for visitors.
☎ 0303 267441

HORSE RIDING

Hayne Barn Riding School
Hayne Barn, Saltwood
General instruction, livery, riding holidays, hacking.
☎ 0303 260338

TENNIS

Record Tennis Centre
Hayne Barn, Saltwood
☎ 0303 265512

Special Interests

ART GALLERIES

Port Lympne House
Wildlife Art Gallery
☎ 0303 264647

GARDENS

Port Lympne House
15 acres of terraced gardens on the southern side of a 20th century mansion.
☎ 0303 264647

HISTORIC BUILDINGS

Lympne Castle
Great Hall, built in 1360, flanked by Norman and mediaeval towers.
☎ 0303 267571

HISTORIC HOUSES

Port Lympne House
20th century mansion in Dutch colonial style with unusual and interesting interiors.
☎ 0303 264647

MUSEUMS

Hythe Local History Room
Oaklands, 1 Stade Street
Cinque Ports display, history of coastal defences and smuggling.
☎ 0303 266152/267111

Lympne Castle
Dolls and reproduction mediaeval brasses.
☎ 0303 267571

Port Lympne House
Wildlife exhibits, ceramics, bronze, ivory and silver.
☎ 0303 264647

RAILWAYS

Romney, Hythe and Dymchurch Railway
14 miles of steam-hauled small gauge railway across Romney Marsh.
☎ 0679 62353

ZOOS

Port Lympne Zoo Park
Wide range of animals and rare breeds; safari rides.
☎ 0303 264647

141

Bewl Water is well worth a visit, whether you want to take a trip on a boat or explore the attractive surrounding countryside. Don't miss Scotney Castle and Gardens and remember to try the local wines and smoked produce.

Population 1350

Outdoor Leisure

CAMPING AND CARAVANNING

Cedar Gables
On the A21 midway between
Lamberhurst and Flimwell
Small site; 5 pitches for caravans,
10 pitches for tents.
☎ 0892 890566

FISHING

Game Fishing

Bartley Mill Trout Fishery
Bartley Mill, Bellsyeu Green, near Frent
Working watermill offers fishing, lovely
walks and falconry; tea room, shop.

Bewl Water
Large reservoir with an excellent trout
fishery. Trout fishing April to October
only, telephone the fishing lodge for
details.
☎ 0892 890352

GOLF

Lamberhurst Golf Club ⓘ
Church Road
Visitors welcome with a reservation.
☎ 0892 890241

Special Interests

ARTS AND CRAFTS

**Mr Heaver's Noted Model Museum and
Craft Village**
Forstal Farm
Upper floors of oast house hold old
English street craft centre.
☎ 0892 890711

Hook Green Pottery
Hook Green
Hand-made stoneware and porcelain.
☎ 0892 890504

142

COUNTRY PARKS

Bewl Water
The largest area of inland water in
south-east England set in attractive
countryside. Waterside walks, boat
trips, sailing, fishing, an adventure
playground, visitor centre and special
events.
☎ 0892 890661

FOOD AND DRINK

Lamberhurst Vineyard
Ridge Farm
Largest vineyard in the south east. Own
label wine, locally made liqueur and
liqueur chocolates available.
☎ 0892 890844/890286

The Weald Smokery
Mount Farm, Flimwell
Smoked fish and meats.
☎ 0580 87601

GARDENS

Emmetts
Ide Hill
Year-round displays at one of the highest
gardens in Kent.
☎ 0892 890651

Scotney Castle Gardens
Created in the 1840s around 14th
century castle ruins. National Trust.
☎ 0892 890651

Sprivers Gardens
Horsmonden
Naturally set garden with a variety of
plants and shrubs. Woodland walks.
☎ 0892 890651

HERITAGE

Bayham Abbey
Remains of church, gatehouse and
ecclesiastical buildings. Also ruins of
house of monks founded in 1208 and
dissolved in 1525.
☎ 0892 890381

Old Soar Manor
Borough Green
Remains of 13th century knight's
dwelling.
☎ 0892 890651

Scotney Castle
Ruins of small 14th century moated castle. Hussey family exhibition; open-air drama.
☎ 0892 890651

HISTORIC BUILDINGS

Bartley Mill
Fully restored working watermill.
☎ 0892 890372

MUSEUMS

Mr Heaver's Noted Model Museum and Craft Village
Converted oast house with model museum, diorama and craft centre.
☎ 0892 890711

Water Sports

BOAT TRIPS

Bewl Water
45-minute cruises on the *Frances Mary*; April to October only.
☎ 0892 890661

YACHTING

Bewl Water
☎ 0892 890661

Leatherhead is an attractive old town on the River Mole. Some fine buildings can be seen in its narrow streets including an early 16th century coaching inn. Sir Anthony Hawkins (Anthony Hope) who wrote *Prisoner of Zenda*, is buried in the parish churchyard.

Market day Friday
Early closing Wednesday
Population 9700

Aerial Sports

MICROLIGHT FLYING

The Surrey Microlight Club
Little Bookham
Contact John Parker.
☎ 0372 458321

Indoor Sports

BADMINTON

Leatherhead Leisure Centre
☎ 0372 377674

LEISURE CENTRES

Leatherhead Leisure Centre
Guildford Road
☎ 0372 377674

SQUASH

Leatherhead Leisure Centre
☎ 0372 377674

Outdoor Leisure

FISHING

Coarse Fishing
Fishing on the Thames. For information and permits contact the National Rivers Authority, Thames Region.
☎ 0734 535000

GOLF

Effingham Golf Club ⛳
Effingham
Visitors welcome, with a reservation, Tuesday afternoon to Friday.
☎ 0372 452203

Leatherhead Golf Club ⛳
Kingston Road
Phone for information about visitor restrictions.
☎ 0372 843966

HORSE RIDING

Vale Lodge Stables
Downs Lane, off Dorking Road
Instruction in riding and jumping.
☎ 0372 373184

143

Special Interests

HISTORIC BUILDINGS

St Mary & St Nicholas
11th century church with prominent tower set askew to provide space for processions along an ancient right of way.

St Nicholas' Church
Off the A246 at Great Bookham
Interesting church with a 12th century nave and a Saxon window. Keyholders' address on door if closed.

MUSEUMS

Fire and Iron Gallery
Oxshott Road

Exhibitions of ornamental metalwork manufactured by blacksmiths from around the world.
☎ 0372 375148

Leatherhead Museum of Local History
Hampton Cottage, 64 Church Street
17th century building containing history of Leatherhead and District up to the present day.
☎ 0372 458722

THEATRES

Thorndike Theatre
Church Street
☎ 0372 377677

KENT   Leeds   KENT

Dating from the 12th century Leeds Castle is constructed on two islands in a lake set in picturesque landscaped parkland. Said to be the favourite country home of Edward I and Queen Eleanor, it was occupied by a number of queens including Henry VIII's first wife, Catherine of Aragon. It was also the home of French and Dutch prisoners of war during the 17th century. Other notable buildings in the charming village include the 14th century, stone-built Battle Hall, and the church, which carries a massive Norman tower.

Leeds Castle

Outdoor Leisure

GOLF

Leeds Castle Golf Course ⏏₁₈
Leeds Castle
Set in the grounds of Leeds Castle. Visitors with correct dress welcome with prior booking.
☎ 0622 880467

Special Interests

ARTS AND CRAFTS

Kent Garden Costume Dolls
Yew Tree House, Upper Street
Manufacture of reproduction antique porcelain dolls.
☎ 0622 861638

FACTORY TOURS

Kent Garden Costume Dolls
☎ 0622 861638

Kent Garden Vineyard
Yew Tree House, Upper Street
Vineyard and winery, wine sales.
☎ 0622 861638

FESTIVALS AND FAIRS

November
Fireworks at Leeds Castle
☎ 0622 765400

GARDENS

Leeds Castle
Parkland, gardens, maze; ducks and
other birds.
☎ 0622 765400

HERITAGE

Sutton Valence Castle
On the A274
Ruins of a 12th century stone keep.
English Heritage.

HISTORIC BUILDINGS

Church of St Nicholas
Massive early Norman tower; 15th
century rood screen.

Leeds Castle
This spectacular castle dates from the
9th century and is built on two islands in
a lake. Restored 1920s. Collections of
art, furniture and tapestries.
☎ 0622 765400

MUSEUMS

Dog Collar Museum
Leeds Castle
Unique collection.
☎ 0622 765400

THEATRE

Leeds Castle
Open-air concerts and other productions.
☎ 0622 765400

SUSSEX / Lewes / SUSSEX

A castle keep and barbican dominate the ancient town of Lewes which has
well-preserved houses in steep streets linked by narrow passageways known as
twittens. Built in 1101 by William the Conqueror's son-in-law, William de Warenne,
the castle looks down on the South Downs and the valley of the River Ouse. De
Warenne also built the Priory of St Pancras, from which stones were taken to build
Southover Grange after the Dissolution of Monasteries in 1537. Some of the biggest
bonfire celebrations in England are held here – bonfires and torchlight processions.

i 32 High Street
☎ 0273 483448

Market days Monday, Tuesday
Early closing Wednesday
Population 14,971

Aerial Sports

GLIDING

East Sussex Gliding Club
Kitsons Field, The Brayle, Ringmer
☎ 0825 840347

Outdoor Leisure

GOLF

Lewes Golf Club ⊩₁₈
Chapel Hill
Visitors welcome.
☎ 0273 473245

HORSE RIDING

Crockstead Equestrian Centre
Crockstead Farm, Halland
Private tuition, competition centre and
livery. Weekend breaks.
☎ 0825 840797

Special Interests

ANTIQUES

Pastorale Antiques
15 Malling Street
☎ 0273 473259

Young Lionel Antiques
1 South Street
☎ 0273 472455

ART GALLERIES

Bentley Wildfowl and Motor Museum
Bentley, Halland
Philip Rickman Collection of wildfowl paintings.
☎ 0825 840573

Firle Place
Firle
Collection of old masters, contemporary local artists, specialist porcelain and furniture.
☎ 0273 858335

ARTS AND CRAFTS

The Old Needlemakers
West Street
Arcade of small craft shops in converted 19th century candle factory.
☎ 071 836 7580

Mary Potter Studio
Hunters Wood, Laughton
☎ 0825 840438

FESTIVALS AND FAIRS

November
Bonfire celebrations at Lewes Castle.

GARDENS

Southover Grange Gardens
Southover Road
Old world gardens of a 16th century house, boyhood home of diarist John Evelyn.
☎ 0273 471600

HERITAGE

Lewes Castle
The shell of a Norman keep. Restored 14th century barbican gateway.
☎ 0273 474379

HISTORIC HOUSES

Charleston Farmhouse
Firle
Once home to members of the 'Bloomsbury Set' with original decorations by the artists themselves.
☎ 0321 83265

Firle Place
Firle
Tudor and Georgian house, home of the Gage family for over 500 years.
☎ 0273 858335

Monks House
Rodmell
Home of Virginia and Leonard Woolf from 1919 to 1969.
☎ 0273 472385

MUSEUMS

Anne of Cleves House Museum
Southover High Street
Old timber-framed house with items and displays portraying Sussex life from centuries ago.
☎ 0273 474610

Bentley Wildfowl and Motor Museum
The largest private collection of rare wildfowl in England. Also collection of roadworthy Edwardian and vintage cars. Miniature steam railway.
☎ 0825 840573

Lewes Living History Model
Barbican House, 169 High Street
Living history display of Lewes with *son et lumière*.
☎ 0273 474379

Military Heritage Museum
7-9 West Street
☎ 0273 473137

Museum of Sussex Archaeology
Barbican House, 169 High Street
Elizabethan dwelling houses displays portraying impact of invaders, including Romans and Normans.
☎ 0273 474379

RAILWAYS

Bentley Wildfowl and Motor Museum
Miniature steam railway.
☎ 0825 84573

WILDLIFE PARKS

Bentley Wildfowl and Motor Museum
The largest private collection of rare wildfowl in England. Philip Rickman Collection of Wildfowl Paintings.
☎ 0825 840573

Raysted Centre for Animal Welfare
On the B2192 at Ringmer
40-acre wildlife sanctuary.
☎ 0825 840252

Water Sports

SWIMMING

The Pells
Brook Street
Large open-air pool.
☎ 0273 472334

Lingfield still has a number of old houses plus a restored cross and a quaint village lock-up. The church, largely rebuilt in the 15th century, has a collection of interesting monuments, brasses and carved stalls.

Outdoor Leisure

GOLF

Lingfield Park Golf Club 🏌️
Racecourse Road, Lingfield Park
Visitors welcome on weekdays and after 1.30 pm at the weekend, driving range open to the public, putting green and practice ground.
☎ 0342 834602

HORSE RACING

Lingfield Park Racecourse Limited
10 furlong triangular course founded in 1890. New all weather track hosts 39 of the 68 race days each year.
☎ 0342 834800

HORSE RIDING

Little Brook Equestrian Centre
East Park Lane, Newchapel
Specialist teaching, small classes, student training and livery.
☎ 0342 832360

Oldencraig Equestrian Centre
Oldencraig Farm, Tandridge Lane, Blindley Heath
Instructional courses, novice jumping, livery, dressage and RDA.
☎ 0342 893317

Special Interests

HISTORIC HOUSES

Great Manor
Ford Manor Road, Dormansland
Fine Victorian manor house.
☎ 0342 832577

Littlehampton is an ancient port situated at the mouth of the River Arun. Relax on the flat, shingle and sand beaches, which have dunes west of the river, or visit the growing marina. There is fishing on the river towpath and boat trips on the river. The Sussex Downs are a short walk away inland and there is an unspoilt 13th century village church nearby.

ℹ ✳ Windmill Complex
Coastguard Road
☎ 0903 713480

Early closing Wednesday
Population 22,181

Indoor Sports

BADMINTON

The Badminton & Squash Club
Sparks Court
☎ 0903 713217

Outdoor Leisure

CAMPING AND CARAVANNING

White Rose Touring Park
Mill Lane, Wick
☎ 0903 716176

FISHING

Sea Fishing
Contact the Tourist Information Centre.
☎ 0903 713480

147

GOLF

Littlehampton Golf Club
Rope Walk
☎ 0903 717170

TENNIS

Maltravers Leisure Park
☎ 0903 726005

The Sportsground
☎ 0903 715109

WALKING AND RAMBLING

There are many opportunities for walks
in and around Littlehampton.
Leaflets are available from the Tourist
Information Centre; they include
Littlehampton History Trail and
Clymping Circular Walk.

Special Interests

ANTIQUES

Joan's Antiques
1 New Road
☎ 0903 722422

ART GALLERIES

Littlehampton Maritime Museum
12a River Road
Two rooms of paintings, plus
photographs and maps.
☎ 0903 715149

FESTIVALS AND FAIRS

July
Littlehampton Carnvial

FUN PARKS

Smarts Amusement Park
☎ 0903 721200

MUSEUMS

Littlehampton Maritime Museum
Local history of Littlehampton,
archaeology, exhibits, maps and
photographs.
☎ 0903 715149

THEATRES

The Windmill
The Green
☎ 0903 724929

Water Sports

BOAT TRIPS

River Arun Cruises
Launch cruises in Arun Valley with
stops at Arundel and Amberley.
☎ 0903 883920

DIVING

Arun Divers
☎ 0903 783541

SWIMMING

Swimming & Sports Centre
☎ 0903 725451

WINDSURFING

Angmering Windsurfing
Western Promenade
☎ 0903 850031

YACHTING

Littlehampton Marina
Ferry Road
☎ 0903 713553

KENT / Lullingstone KENT

Lullingstone, near Eynsford in North Kent, is notable for its 18th century castle and
more recently, the Brands Hatch circuit.

Adventure Sports

SHOOTING

**Brands Hatch Circuit and Activity
Centre**
☎ 0474 872367

Aerial Sports

PARAGLIDING

**Brands Hatch Circuit and Activity
Centre**
☎ 0474 872367

Multi-Activity Holidays

Brands Hatch Circuit and Activity Centre
Famous motor racing circuit and racing school; parascending; go-karting; clay pigeon shooting and driving.
☎ 0474 872331/872367

Racing at Brands Hatch

Special Interests

HERITAGE

Eynsford Castle
Eynsford
11th century castle ruins.
☎ 0892 548166

Lullingstone Roman Villa
Lullingstone Lane, Eynsford
Villa built in 1st century and occupied until 5th century. Extensive mosaics have now been excavated.
☎ 0322 863467

HISTORIC HOUSES

Lullingstone Castle
Historic mansion, frequently visited by Henry VIII, still run by descendants of the original owners.
☎ 0322 862114

KENT — **Lydd** — KENT

Lydd lies 3 miles inland but was once a coastal town. Its partly 14th century church has an impressive tower and is known as the 'Cathedral of Romney Marsh'. The explosive 'Lyddite' was first tested here and takes its name from the town.

Aerial Sports

FLYING

London Flight Centre
Lydd Airport, Romney Marsh
All levels catered for.
☎ 0679 21549

South East College of Air Training
Lydd Airport, Romney Marsh
Pleasure flights. Commercial and private pilot training offered.
☎ 0679 21236

Outdoor Leisure

WALKING & RAMBLING

Romney Marsh Walks
A series of circular walks. Contact the Shepway District Council.
☎ 0303 850388

Special Interests

HISTORIC BUILDINGS

All Saints Church
Fine 13th to 14th century building with a striking 15th century tower. The 'Cathedral of Romney Marsh'.

Water Sports

WATER SKIING

Lydd Water Ski Club
Dengmarsh Road
☎ 022 745 5750 Secretary

WINDSURFING

Romney Marsh Windsurfing Centre
Dengmarsh Road
Windsurfing and canoe hire.
☎ 0679 21028

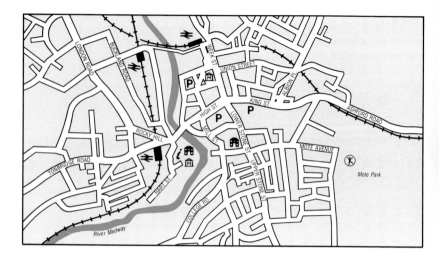

Maidstone straddles the Rivers Medway and Len and occupies the heart of the rich Kent farmland known as 'the garden of England'. The town has sent fruit and vegetables to London since the Middle Ages and continues this tradition today. It is also the principal source of hops for the nation's brewing industries. Amongst its mediaeval buildings are the Archbishop's Palace, the Church of All Saints and the College of Secular Canons. The early 15th century Archbishop's Stables now house a carriage museum. The family of Thomas Wyatt, who led the Protestant Insurrection in 1554, owned Chillington Manor House in Faith's Street which is now the town museum and art gallery. The Wyatts also owned Allington Castle which was built in the 13th century on a site occupied since Roman times. There are trees, gardens, inviting riverside walks and plenty of opportunities for 'messing about on the river'.

i The Gatehouse
Old Palace Gardens
Mill Street
☎ 0622 673581

Market day Tuesday
Early closing Wednesday
Population 87,068

Aerial Sports

FLYING

London Flight Centre
Headcorn Airfield
Pleasure flights and trial lessons.
☎ 0622 890997

PARACHUTING

Slipstream Adventures
Headcorn Airfield
Full instruction courses.
☎ 0622 890641/890862

Indoor Sports

LEISURE CENTRES

Maidstone Leisure Centre
Mote Park
Extensive facilities including health and fitness suite. Due to open spring 1991.
☎ 0622 761111 for information

Westborough Sports Centre
Oakwood Park, Tonbridge Road
Multi-gym, solarium, keep-fit, squash courts.
☎ 0622 759615

YMCA Sports Centre
Melrose Close, off Cripple Street
☎ 0622 743317

SQUASH

Westborough Sports Centre
☎ 0622 759615

150

Multi-Activity Holidays

SPECIAL INTEREST CENTRES

Kent Institute of Art and Design
Oakwood Park
Week-long summer arts courses for young people. Contact Jane Seaman.
☎ 0622 757286

TENNIS

Record Tennis Centre
Mill Meadow, St Peter's Street
☎ 0622 681987

Westborough Sports Centre
Floodlit courts.
☎ 0622 759615

WALKING AND RAMBLING

A Walk around Maidstone
Contact the Tourist Information Centre for details and leaflets.

Outdoor Leisure

FISHING

Coarse Fishing
Fishing on the River Medway at Maidstone and Wateringbury.
☎ 0233 84674
☎ 0622 813927

Abbey Court Lake
Sandling
Day tickets avilable.
☎ 0622 690318 after 6 pm

Mote Park Lake
Contact the Tourist Information Centre.
☎ 0622 602169

GOLF

Bearsted Golf Course
Ware Street, Bearsted
Secluded parkland course with views of North Downs. Telephone for details of restrictions.
☎ 0622 38389

Cobtree Manor Park Golf Club ⌐₁₈
Chatham Road, Sandling
Municipal course. Visitors welcome with prior booking.
☎ 0622 753276

West Malling Golf Club ⌐₁₈
London Road
Visitors welcome weekdays and weekend mornings.
☎ 0732 844022

HORSE RIDING

Horseshoes Riding School
Dean Street, East Farleigh
General instruction, hacking, non-residential holiday courses.
☎ 0622 746161

Lower Bell Riding School
Back Lane, Boughton Monchelsea
☎ 0622 745906

Special Interests

ART GALLERIES

Maidstone Museum and Art Gallery
St Faith's Street
☎ 0622 754497

ARTS AND CRAFTS

Mill Yard Craft Centre
West Malling
☎ 0732 843484

Whitbread Hop Farm Craft Centre
Beltring, Paddock Wood
Assorted crafts; farrier, cartwright, cowlmakers and cricket ball workshop.
☎ 0622 872068/872408

COUNTRY PARKS

Cobtree Manor Park
Sandling

Haysden Country Park
Off the A26
160-acre park with two lakes.
☎ 0732 844522

Mote Park
450-acre park with lake, nature trail and walks.
☎ 0622 673581

Feeding the swans at Mote Park

FACTORY VISITS

Whitbread Hop Farm Craft Centre
☎ 0622 872068/872408

FARM PARKS

Whitbread Hop Farm
Beltring, Paddock Wood
Preserved oast houses and barns, hop
fields, machinery, Whitbread Shire
Horses and local crafts.
☎ 0622 872068

FESTIVALS AND FAIRS

June
International Balloon Festival

July
Maidstone Carnival
Maidstone River Festival

August
Maidstone Festival

September
Maidstone Beer Festival
North Kent Festival of Cultures

FOOD AND DRINK

Bearsted Vineyard
24 Caring Lane, Bearsted
4 acres of vines. Guided tours.
☎ 0622 36974

Headcorn Vineyard
Grigg Lane, Headcorn
Vineyard and flower nursery. Guided
tours, shop.
☎ 0622 890561

HERITAGE

Kits Coty
2 miles north of Maidstone off the A229
Framework of two Megalithic tombs,
formerly covered by earthen mounds.

HISTORIC BUILDINGS

Allington Castle
Castle Road, Allington
Moated 13th century castle with a
gatehouse and courtyard, on the River
Medway. Collections of furniture, art
and sculpture. Now belongs to
Carmelite Order.
☎ 0622 754080

All Saints' Church
Mill Street
14th century perpendicular church.

Archbishops' Palace
Mill Street
15th century stables now house the
Tyrwhitt-Drake Museum of Carriages.

*Archbishops' Palace and the River
Medway*

The Friars
Aylesford
Carmelite Friary founded here in 1240;
now an important pilgrimage centre.
☎ 0622 717272

HISTORIC HOUSES

Boughton Monchelsea Place
Boughton Monchelsea
1567 Elizabethan manor with Regency
alterations. Collections of clothing,
vehicles and farm implements, deer
park, tea rooms.
☎ 0622 743120

Stoneacre
Otham
15th century half-timbered manor house
with garden. Embroidery exhibition.
National Trust.
☎ 0622 861861

MUSEUMS

Maidstone Museum and Art Gallery
Local history housed in former
Chillington Manor House.
☎ 0622 754497

Museum of Kent Rural Life
Lock Lane, Cobtree Manor Park,
Sandling
Oast houses and 27 acres of land with
displays relating to rural life. Craft
demonstrations, special events.
Refreshments, childrens playground,
shop.
☎ 0622 763936

**Museum of the Queen's Own Royal
West Kent Regiment**
St Faith's Street
Newly restored museum with uniforms,
weapons, medals, pictures and other
artefacts.
☎ 0622 754497

Carriage Museum

Tyrwhitt-Drake Museum of Carriages
Mill Street
Large collection of horse-drawn vehicles,
restored to their original state.
☎ 0622 754497

Whitbread Hop Farm
Preserved oast houses and barns, hop
fields, machinery, Whitbread Shire
horses and local crafts.
☎ 0622 872068

RAILWAYS

Mote Park
Miniature railway rides on Sunday
afternoons in summer.
☎ 0622 673581

THEATRES

Hazlitt Theatre
Earl Street
☎ 0622 758611

Water Sports

BOAT HIRE

Tovil Bridge Boatyard
Beaconsfield Road, Tovil
Narrow boats, cruisers, motor dinghies
and rowing boats for hire.
☎ 0622 686341

BOAT TRIPS

Kentish Lady II
Undercliffe Boathouse, Bishops Way
Hourly boat trips on the Medway.
☎ 0622 753740

SWIMMING

Maidstone Leisure Centre
Leisure pool, wave machine and flumes.
Due to open Spring 1991.
☎ 0622 761111 for information

Mote Baths
Mote Park
☎ 0622 764631

The bathing machine was invented by a local Quaker in 1753 and this, coupled with Margate's nine miles of sandy beaches helped to establish the town as a desirable location at the very start of the seaside industry. With easy access from London, Margate continues to flourish today while preserving many of its Regency and Victorian buildings. The inland local grotto has shells said to have been placed there over 2000 years ago.

i Marine Terrace
☎ 0843 220241

Market day Monday
Early closing Thursday
Population 54,980

Aerial Sports

MICROLIGHT FLYING

Kent Microlight and Aircraft Club
Contact M Baldwin.
☎ 0843 590604

Indoor Sports

BADMINTON

Hartsdown Park Sports and Leisure Centre
☎ 0843 226221

Lonsdale Court Sports Centre
Norfolk Road, Cliftonville
☎ 0843 221053

LEISURE CENTRES

Hartsdown Park Sports and Leisure Centre
Behind the railway station
☎ 0843 226221

SQUASH

Dreamland Squash Club
Marine Terrace
☎ 0843 226578

TEN PIN BOWLING

Top Ten Bowling
Cliftonville sea front
☎ 0843 228632

Multi-Activity Holidays

SPECIAL INTEREST CENTRES

Garden of England Cycling Holidays
Barn Cottage, Harbourland, Boxley
Variable length cycling holidays,
bicycles supplied if required.
☎ 0622 675891

Outdoor Leisure

CYCLING

The Bike Shed
Canterbury Road, Westbrook
☎ 0843 228866

Ken's Bike Shop
26 Eaton Road
☎ 0843 221422

FISHING

Sea Fishing
Contact the Tourist Information
Centre.
☎ 0843 220241

TENNIS

Hartsdown Park
4 tennis courts.
☎ 0843 224055

Special Interests

HERITAGE

Margate Caves
Entrance on 1 Northdown Road
Caves of cathedral-like dimensions
hewn out of chalk in Saxon times.
☎ 0843 220139

Clock Tower, Margate

Carousel at Bemboms

HISTORIC BUILDINGS

Drapers Mill
St Peters Footpath, College Road
1850 smock mill restored to working order; museum room.
☎ 0843 291696

Salmestone Grange
Nash Road
Mediaeval monastic grange with 14th century chapel and 20th century stained glass windows.
☎ 0843 220909

Sarre Windmill
Canterbury Road, Sarre
Working mill, craft shop, traction engine, animal corner and cider press.
☎ 0843 47573

Shell Grotto
Entrance off Northdown Road
Accidentally discovered in 1835, its origin is still a mystery.
☎ 0843 220008

HISTORIC HOUSES

Quex House and Gardens
Off the A28 near Birchington
Thanet's only stately home; Regency with Victorian additions. Collections of furniture, paintings and Chinese porcelain.
0843 42168

MUSEUMS

Old Town Hall Local History Museum
Local history of 18th and 19th centuries. Victorian police station and court room.
0843 225511 extn 2520

Powell Cotton Museum
Quex Park, Birchington
Natural history and ethnography, diorama of Asian and African animals.
☎ 0843 42166

Quex House Museum
Quex Park, Birchington
Nine gallery, purpose-built museum. Internationally important collections.
☎ 0843 42168

Tudor House and Museum
King Street
Oldest domestic building in Margate (16th century); contains local history exhibits.
☎ 0843 225511 extn 2520

THEATRES

Theatre Royal
The second oldest theatre in Britain.
☎ 0843 221913

Tom Thumb Theatre
The smallest stage in the world.
☎ 0843 221791

Winter Gardens Theatre
☎ 0843 296111/292795

THEME PARKS

Bembom Brothers White Knuckle Theme Park
Assorted rides for all the family.
☎ 0843 227011

Water Sports

CANOEING

Thanet Canoe Club
Newgate Gap, Cliftonville
☎ 0843 225580

JET-SKIING

Water Sports International
Palm Bay, Cliftonville
☎ 0843 226079

SWIMMING

Hartsdown Park Sports and Leisure Centre
'Sea serpents' flumes.
☎ 0843 226221

WATER-SKIING

Forenesse Water-Ski Club
Forenesse Bay, Cliftonville
☎ 0843 61071

155

Minster is the highest point on the Isle of Sheppey – a small island at the mouth of the River Medway, separated from the mainland by a narrow branch of the sea called 'The Swale'. The resort has extensive views over the Thames and Medway estuaries and a pleasant sand and shingle beach. It takes its name from an ancient Saxon nunnery, which was sacked by Danish invaders in 835. Parts of this building survived the raid and were incorporated into Minster Abbey. The restored church contains many interesting items including an effigy of Sir Robert Shurland and some 14th century brasses.

Early closing Wednesday
Population 10,800

Outdoor Leisure

CAMPING AND CARAVANNING

Horseshoe Caravan Park
Bell Farm Lane
Small site, welcomes tents and caravans.
☎ 0795 872446

Leysdown Coastal Park Camp Site
Shellness Road, Leysdown
New site for touring caravans with comprehensive facilities.

Seacliff Holiday Estates
Oak Lane
40 pitches for tents, touring or motor caravans.
☎ 0795 872262

HORSE RIDING

Taylor's Riding Establishment
Casita, Waverley Avenue
☎ 0795 872203

Special Interests

Minster Abbey Gatehouse

HISTORIC BUILDINGS

Harty Church
One of Kent's most remote churches, reached by a narrow lane winding across the marshes.
☎ 0795 510204

Minster Abbey
Twin churches and a Benedictine nunnery gatehouse.
☎ 0795 872303/873720

St Mary and Sexburga
Twin church.

MUSEUMS

Minster Abbey and Gatehouse Museu
Local history including fossils, tools a photographs and magnificent views fr 200-foot-high battlements. Guided tou by arrangement.
☎ 0795 872303/873720

NATURAL HISTORY

Leysdown Coastal Park
Nature trail and picnic facilities.

156

Until the end of the 13th century, this town was an important Cinque Port, but a violent storm in 1287 destroyed the harbour and changed the course of the River Rother. Before this natural disaster, ships would anchor close to the majestic Church of St Nicholas, now about a mile away from the sea. The church has an impressive Norman tower, an imposing nave and interesting brasses. One way to see Romney Marsh is to take a trip on the steam railway which has a station at New Romney. The station also houses an interesting collection of railway memorabilia and a good model railway display.

i ✳ 2 Littlestone Road
☎ 0679 64044

Market day Friday
Early closing Wednesday
Population 4100

Outdoor Leisure

CAMPING AND CARAVANNING

New Romney Caravan Sites Ltd
136A Coast Drive
50 pitches for touring and motor caravans.
☎ 0679 62247

GOLF

Littlestone Golf Club ⁛ ⁌
Littlestone
Visitors welcome.
☎ 0679 62231

Special Interests

ARTS AND CRAFTS

Philippine Craft Centre
Old RAF Camp Site on Romney Marsh
-acre site with craft shops containing over 2000 different handicrafts, cane furniture and clothing from the Philippines. British Craft section opening Spring 1991.
067 94 616

FARM PARKS

Dunrobin Stud
Dunes Road, Greatstone
Shire horses, thoroughbreds, farm animals and harness room on view. Tea room.
0679 63335

HISTORIC BUILDINGS

Newchurch Church
Forlorn church with an overgrown graveyard which epitomises the churches of the Romney Marsh.

New Romney Church
12th century church with a massive tower, an excellent example of Norman masonry.

Old Romney Church
Built from the 13th century onwards; the box pews are painted pink.

Snave Church
On the A2070 at Snave
Another of the desolate churches of Romney Marsh; only accessible by foot; it has a whitewashed interior.

RAILWAYS

Romney, Hythe and Dymchurch Railway
New Romney Station
14 miles of 15-inch gauge steam railway across Romney Marsh. Indoor exhibition, engine shed, café.
☎ 0679 62353

View across Romney Marsh

157

Newhaven

Linked to Dieppe by cross-Channel ferry, Newhaven has another interesting association with France. Louis Philippe and his queen stayed at the Bridge Hotel after the French Revolution.

Early closing Wednesday
Population 10,773

Indoor Sports

LEISURE CENTRES

Meridian Leisure Centre
Peacehaven
Sports hall, conditioning room, sunbeds.
☎ 0273 587803

Tideway Leisure Centre
Southdown Road
☎ 0273 517601

Outdoor Leisure

FISHING

Sea Fishing
Contact the Tourist Information Centre.

GOLF

Peacehaven Golf Club ⓑ
The Clubhouse, Brighton Road
Visitors welcome without reservation.
☎ 0273 514049

TENNIS

Tideway Leisure Centre
☎ 0273 517601

Special Interests

GARDENS

Tate's Garden Paradise
Avis Road
Landscape gardens with walk-through waterfall, lakes and miniature railway.
☎ 0273 512123

HISTORIC BUILDINGS

Newhaven Fort
Fort Road
Victorian coastal fort built for Lord Palmerston in the 1860s.
☎ 0273 517622

MUSEUMS

Newhaven Fort
Military museum, barrack rooms, underground tunnels and galleries.
☎ 0273 517622

Water Sports

SWIMMING

Seahaven Pool
Town centre
25-metre pool.
☎ 0273 512498

Winter Sports

SKIING

Borowski Ski Centre
New Road
Large dry-ski slope. Lessons; ski shop, workshop, bar.
☎ 0273 515402

The South Downs

Situated on the Thames, Northfleet offers a wide choice of recreational facilities. The 14th century screen in St Botolph's Church is said to be the oldest in Kent.

Indoor Sports

LEISURE CENTRES

Cygnet Leisure Centre
Old Perry Street
☎ 0474 337484

Outdoor Leisure

TENNIS

Wombwell Park
Mitchell Avenue

Special Interests

FESTIVALS AND FAIRS

July
Northfleet Carnival

HISTORIC BUILDINGS

Our Lady of the Assumption
Built in 1914 by Sir Gilbert Scott in the 'new' mediaeval style.

St Botolphs
A fine 14th century church, one of the largest parish churches in Kent. Interesting monumental brasses.

MUSEUMS

Blue Circle Heritage Centre
The history of the manufacture of cement in the area housed in the oldest existing cement works. Model rail system; display of cement bags.
☎ 0474 323598

Water Sports

SWIMMING

Cygnet Leisure Centre
☎ 0474 337477

Northfleet Pool
25-metre, 6-lane pool; learner pool; diving area.
☎ 0474 337484

The River Thames at nearby Gravesend

This charming town is characterised by cobbled streets and fine old buildings. Visit Market Place, Saddler's Row and East Street.

Population 2973

Outdoor Leisure

CAMPING AND CARAVANNING

Camping and Caravanning Club Site
Great Bury, Graffham
90 pitches; good facilities.
☎ 079 86 476 before 8 pm

FISHING

Coarse Fishing

Coultershaw Mill
Fittleworth
Day tickets available from local tackle shops.

GOLF

Cowdray Park Country Club ⛳
Midhurst
Visitors welcome at weekends, after 11 am only.
☎ 0730 812091

Special Interests

ART GALLERIES

Petworth House
Turner, Van Dyke, Gainsborough, Reynolds and other notable works housed in an impressive 17th century house.
☎ 0798 42207

FACTORY VISITS

Lurgashall Winery
Windfallwood Common, Lurgashall
See all the stages in the making of wine, mead and liqueurs. Visitor centre, museum and shop.
☎ 0428 78292

FARM PARKS

Noah's Farmyard
Grittenham Farm, Tillington
Children's farm visits.
☎ 079 85 264

FOOD AND DRINK

Lurgashall Winery
☎ 0428 78292

GARDENS

Petworth House Park
Gardens landscaped by Capability Brown; deer park.
☎ 0798 42207

HISTORIC HOUSES

Petworth House
Magnificent late-17th century house with fine collections of paintings and furniture. Painted by Turner who was a constant visitor in the 1830's.
☎ 0798 42207

MUSEUMS

Lurgashall Winery
☎ 0428 78292

When the Normans landed here in 1066, they found a ready-made Roman wall from the time of an earlier occupation. They built their own castle within these well-preserved walls and the remains of both can be seen today. Pevensey Bay has shingle beach with sand at low tide.

i ✳ Castle car park
☎ 0323 761444

Early closing Thursday
Population 2668

Outdoor Leisure

CAMPING AND CARAVANNING

Camping and Caravanning Club Site
Normans Bay
250 pitches; good facilities; private
beach.
☎ 0323 761190 before 8 pm

FISHING

Coarse Fishing
For information and permits for fishing
at Pevensey Levels contact the National
Rivers Authority.
☎ 0732 838858

Special Interests

HERITAGE

Pevensey Castle
Mediaeval castle, including the remains
of an unusual keep, enclosed within the
walls of a 4th century Roman fort. The
castle has a turbulent history; it was
attacked four times between 1066 and
the 14th century, was refortified against
the Spanish Armada and again during
World War Two.

The Filching Manor Motor Museum is well worth a visit for its fine collection of
veteran and vintage cars. Other attractions include walking and horse riding.

Outdoor Leisure

HORSE RIDING

Cophall Farm Stables
Eastbourne Road
Holiday instruction. Riding holidays for
children aged 10 to 15.
☎ 0321 23975

Gatewood Stables
Off the A27 to Lewes
☎ 0321 23709

WALKING AND RAMBLING

The Arlington Bluebell Walk
Bates Green Farm, Arlington
Five walks around a conservation farm.
☎ 0321 25151

Special Interests

MUSEUMS

Filching Manor Motor Museum
Jevington Road, Wannock
15th century hall house with a
collection of veteran, vintage, sports
and racing cars. Also the Bluebird K3
speedboat in which Sir Malcolm

Campbell broke the world speed record
in 1937.
☎ 0321 27838/27124

Polegate Windmill and Miller Museum
1817 red brick tower mill, restored in
1967. Museum of milling with models
and photographs.
☎ 0321 24763

161

Pulborough

Pulborough is a small, pleasant town which grew up around crossroads on the old Roman Stone Street, the London to Chichester road. It has some attractive half-timbered and stone-built houses and several old bridges spanning the River Arun. The large church displays a massive 12th century font, and a delightful 14th century lych-gate.

Early closing Wednesday
Population 3223

Multi-Activity Holidays

SPECIAL INTEREST CENTRES

The Old Rectory Adult Education College
Off the A283 at Fittleworth
Wildlife and bird study courses.
☎ 0798 82306

Outdoor Leisure

FISHING

Coarse Fishing
For information and permits contact the National Rivers Authority.
☎ 0323 762691

GOLF

West Sussex Golf Club ⛳₁₈
Horston Warren
Visitors welcome by prior arrangement, except on Tuesdays.
☎ 079 82 2563

HORSE RIDING

Coldwaltham House
Off the A29, 2 miles south of Pulborough
Residential instructional holidays.
☎ 0798 831418

West Sussex College of Agriculture and Horticulture
Brinsbury, North Heath
☎ 0798 23832

Special Interests

FOOD AND DRINK

Nutbourne Manor Vineyard
East of Pulborough at Nutbourne
18-acre vineyard with Domesday mill, millpond and lake. Self-guided tours.
☎ 0798 813554

GARDENS

Parham House Gardens
Parham Park
Well laid-out gardens including walled and 18th century gardens, trees, lake and church.
☎ 0903 742021

HISTORIC HOUSES

Parham House
Striking Elizabethan house with collections of art, china, furniture, needlework, tapestries and carpets.
☎ 0903 742021

MUSEUMS

Bignor Roman Villa
South-west at Bignor
Villa remains with some of the finest mosaics outside Italy, as well as displays of other artefacts.
☎ 079 87 259

NATURAL HISTORY

The Old Rectory Adult Education College
☎ 0798 82306

Ramsgate

Once a fishing village, Ramsgate developed into a town during the 18th century and its street names are constant reminders of the role it played during the Napoleonic Wars. In fact, Ramsgate has strong connections with many important periods in history. Hengist and Horsa landed here in 449 and St Augustine visited in 597. Ramsgate has served as a Channel port since Roman times and has had a hovercraft terminal since 1969. As well as large commercial vessels, it plays host to much smaller fishing and pleasure craft and these can be seen in the harbour and yacht marina. Sandy, south-facing beaches are sheltered by chalk cliffs and the Esplanade has amusement parks and a pavilion. There is excellent sea-fishing from the harbour and the more adventurous can hire fishing boats for the day.

i The Argyle Centre
Queen Street
☎ 0843 591086

Market day Friday
Early closing Thursday
Population 37,398

Aerial Sports

PARAGLIDING

Seawide Leisure
Western Undercliff
May to September daily from 11 am.
☎ 0843 294144

Indoor Sports

SQUASH

Dumpton Stadium
Hereson Road
☎ 0843 593333

Outdoor Leisure

BIRDWATCHING

Pegwell Bay
miles from Ramsgate
Open land with information boards and
ides. Important staging post for
migratory birds.

CAMPING AND CARAVANNING

Manston Caravan and Camping Park
Manston Court Road, Manston
00 pitches; facilities.
0843 823442

FISHING

Coarse Fishing
For information and permits for fishing on the River Stour contact the National Rivers Authority at Tonbridge.
☎ 0732 838858

Sea Fishing
Contact the Tourist Information Centre for details.
☎ 0843 591086

HORSE RIDING

Nelson Park Riding Centre
Off the A253 at Woodchurch
☎ 0843 822251

TENNIS

Montefiore Avenue
Four tennis courts.
☎ 0843 594804

Warre Recreation Ground
Six tennis courts.
☎ 0843 593754

Special Interests

FESTIVALS AND FAIRS

August
Ramsgate Royal Harbour Heritage Festival

HISTORIC BUILDINGS

St Augustine's Church
1850 church by Gothic revival architect Pugin, who is buried here.

163

MUSEUMS

Agricultural and Rural Life Museum
West at Minster
Farm equipment and traditional crafts.
☎ 0843 225511 extn 2155

East Kent Maritime Museum
The Clock House, Pier Yard, Royal Harbour
Maritime history, wrecks, lifeboats and harbour trail.
☎ 0843 587765

Maritime Museum
Local and national seafaring history.
☎ 0843 587765

Motor Museum
From Penny Farthings to 60s sports cars.
☎ 0843 581948

Ramsgate Museum
Ramsgate Library, Guildford Lawn
Civic life and history of harbour and town; pictures and prints.
☎ 0843 593532

NATURAL HISTORY

Pegwell Bay
Interesting flora and fauna; birdwatching, walks.

Water Sports

WATER-SKIING

Seawide Leisure
Western Undercliff
☎ 0843 294144

SURREY | Reigate | SURREY

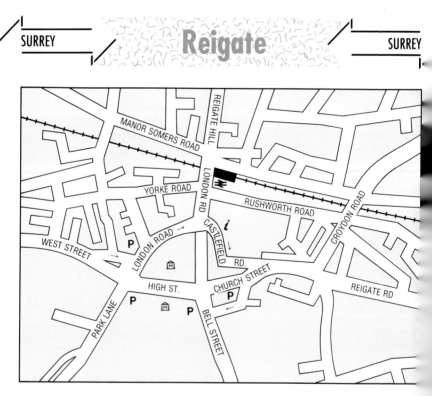

Set in the Surrey Hills, Reigate developed as a market town in the early Middle Ages. You can still see Reigate Castle which was originally the home of the De Warenne family who came over to England with William the Conqueror. Other old buildings include the quaint 18th century Old Town Hall, the 16th century Old Sweep's House in Slipshoe Street and a timber-framed, tile-hung house, La Trobes, in the High Street. The town was once an important coaching stop on the London to Brighton road and flourishes today as a busy commercial and residential town. It offers excellent opportunities for sports, leisure and entertainments. Shopping facilities are good and the surrounding countryside is well worth exploring.

i Town Hall
Reigate
☎ 0737 242477

Early closing Wednesday
Population 48,910

Aerial Sports

FLYING

Redhill Flying Club
Redhill Aerodrome
☎ 0737 822959

Indoor Sports

LEISURE CENTRES

Donyngs Recreation Centre
Linkfield Lane, Redhill
Sports hall, health suite, pool.
☎ 0737 764732

SQUASH

Donyngs Recreation Centre
☎ 0737 764732

Reigate Squash Club
Manor Road
☎ 0737 244204

Outdoor Leisure

FISHING

Coarse Fishing
For information and permits contact the
National Rivers Authority, Thames
Region.
☎ 0734 535000

Whitehall Farm
Rock Lane
☎ 0737 645618

GOLF

Redhill and Reigate Golf Club ⛳
Clarence Lodge, Pendleton Road, Redhill
Wooded course. Visitors welcome most
weekdays; phone to give prior notice at
weekends.
☎ 0737 244433

Reigate Heath Golf Club ⛳
The Clubhouse, Reigate Heath
Visitors welcome weekdays, phone first.
☎ 0737 242610

HORSE RIDING

Orchard Cottage Riding Stable
Babylon Lane, Lower Kingswood
Instruction holidays, day courses.
☎ 0737 241311

WALKING AND RAMBLING

Earlswood Common
Woodland, lakes, boating, fishing.

Redhill Common
Parkland and woodland.

Reigate Heath
130 acres to the west of the town.

Special Interests

GARDENS

Castle Grounds
High Street
Attractively-designed gardens, including
the Baron's Caves.

Priory Park
Parkland and gardens, lake and
woodlands.

HISTORIC BUILDINGS

Church of St Mary Magdalene
Chart Lane
Mediaeval church, burial place of
Admiral Lord Howard of Effingham, who
fought the Spanish Armada.

Old Town Hall
18th century building and local heritage
centre.

Reigate Castle
Mediaeval castle, home of the Earls of
Surrey.

Reigate Priory
Built for the Augustinians, but became
Lord Howard of Effingham's private
residence at the dissolution. Now a
school and museum.

Reigate Tunnel
Designed to ease the Prince Regent's
journeys from London to Brighton, now
pedestrianised.

The Windmill Church
Reigate Heath
The world's only church in a windmill.

MUSEUMS

Reigate and Banstead Heritage Centre
Old Town Hall, High Street
☎ 0737 245264

Reigate Priory Museum
Bell Street
School and museum in 750-year-old building.
☎ 0737 245065

Harlequin Theatre
Warwick Quadrant, Redhill
☎ 0737 773721

NATURAL HISTORY

Laporte Earth's Park Woods Nature Trail
South-east at Nutfield
Trail through naturalised old mineral workings.
☎ 0737 765050

New Pond Farm and Felland Wood
Wild flower reserve.

Water Sports

SWIMMING

Donyngs Recreation Centre
☎ 0737 764732

KENT / Rochester / KENT

Rochester Cathedral

Rochester preserves a wealth of historic buildings and is dominated by its castle, on of the finest Norman keeps in Britain. From this vantage point, you can enjo splendid views over the Medway estuary. Another magnificent building is Rocheste Cathedral, which is the second oldest in England. It houses the ancient *Textu Roffensis*, a code of Anglo-Saxon laws. Evidence of Roman occupation can be seen i the High Street where parts of the mediaeval city walls trace the line of these earl fortifications. Rochester also has strong associations with Charles Dickens; the tow holds a festival in summer to celebrate him. He spent the last years of his life at Ga Hill Place and many of the old buildings in the High Street have a very Dickensia flavour. Visitors will find many craft and antique shops as well as tea rooms, coff shops and old pubs. In addition, Rochester offers a wide range of modern sports ar leisure facilities and the lovely scenery of the North Downs is on the doorstep.

i Eastgate Cottage
High Street
☎ 0634 843666

Market day Friday
Early closing Wednesday
Population 24,402

Aerial Sports

MICROLIGHT FLYING

Medway Microlight Club
Contact Chris Draper.
☎ 0634 270780

Indoor Sports

LEISURE CENTRES

Maidstone Road Sports Centre
☎ 0634 727777

Strood Sports Centre
Watling Street, Strood
☎ 0634 723888

Multi-Activity Holidays

MULTI-ACTIVITY CENTRES

Arethusa Venture Centre
Group courses, 1 day to 2 weeks.
Canoeing, swimming, sailing,
orienteering, climbing and field studies.
☎ 0634 719933

SPECIAL INTEREST CENTRES

Medway Cruising School
48 Hevercroft, Strood
Five day courses in the Thames Estuary
and the quiet, unspoilt waters from
Lower Upnor.
☎ 0634 717050

Outdoor Leisure

BIRDWATCHING

Northward Hill
North of High Halstow village
SPB reserve which includes the largest
heronry in the UK. Details from the
Warden, Swishole Cottage, High
Halstow, Rochester.

CAMPING AND CARAVANNING

Woolmans Wood Tourist Caravan Park
On the B2097 at Bridgewood
60 pitches for caravans and tents.
☎ 0634 867685

GOLF

Deangate Ridge Golf Club ⛳
Off the A228 at Hoo
Visitors welcome, bookings required for
weekends.
☎ 0634 251180

**Rochester and Cobham Park Golf
Club** ⛳
Park Pale
Visitors with handicap certificates
welcome during the week.
☎ 047 482 3658

ORIENTEERING

Arethusa Venture Centre
☎ 0634 719933

TENNIS

Jacksons Recreation Ground
☎ 0634 847739 for bookings

WALKING AND RAMBLING

A Walk Around the City
The City of Rochester Society
☎ 0634 846043 Tours Organiser

North Downs Way
Waymarked walk from Gravesend to
Dover, follow the acorn symbol.

Special Interests

FESTIVALS AND FAIRS

June
Dickens Festival

July
River Festival

August
Norman Rochester

December
Dickensian Christmas

HISTORIC BUILDINGS

Fort Amherst
Georgian fortress from Napoleonic
times with 2500 feet of tunnels.
☎ 0634 847747

Rochester Castle
Large 11th century castle, the tallest Norman keep in England. Excellent views and riverside gardens.
☎ 0634 402276

Rochester Cathedral
The Precinct
Consecrated in 604, present building dates from 1077 with 12th and 14th century additions. Beautifully sculpted 12th century west doorway; chapter room contains early 12th century *Textus Roffensis*, a code of Anglo-Saxon laws.
☎ 0634 843366

Temple Manor
Strood
1240 building with a colourful history.
☎ 0634 718743

Upnor Castle
High Street, Upper Upnor
Elizabethan fort, built 1559, to defend Royal Naval Dockyards.
☎ 0634 718742

MUSEUMS

The Dickens Centre
Eastgate House, High Street
16th century red-brick building with tableaux reconstructing scenes from Dickens' books, details of his life and other displays.
☎ 0634 844176

A tableau at the Dickens Centre

Guildhall Museum
High Street
Local history, naval and military, toys and civic history.
☎ 0634 848717

Six Poor Travellers House
High Street
Founded in 1579 by Watts Charity to accommodate 'six poor travellers'.

Kenneth Bills Rochester Motorcycle Museum
144 High Street
☎ 0634 814165

Guildhall Clock, Rochester

Water Sports

BOAT TRIPS

Invicta Line Cruises
Cruise ship from Rochester to Southend in Essex.
☎ 0634 723619

CANOEING

Arethusa Venture Centre
☎ 0634 719933

SWIMMING

Hundred of Hoo Pool
Main Road
☎ 0634 251588

Strood Sports Centre
☎ 0634 723888

168

Royal approval from Charles I paved the way for the fine building that is the town's heritage today. The Pantiles are a haven for lovers of architecture and antiques, while 'A Day at the Wells' gives a glimpse of the town's prosperity in the 18th century.

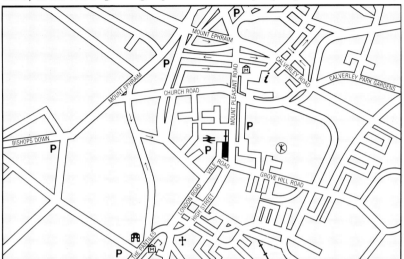

i Monson House
Monson Way
☎ 0892 515675

Indoor Sports

LEISURE CENTRES

Sports and 'Y' Centre
St John's Road
☎ 0892 540744

Multi-Activity Holidays

MULTI-ACTIVITY CENTRES

Bowles Outdoor Centre
Eridge Green
Multi-activity courses for up to seven days, including all adventure sports.
☎ 0892 665665

Outdoor Leisure

FISHING

Coarse Fishing
For information and permits for fishing

Market days Wednesday, Saturday
Early closing Wednesday
Population 58,141

on the River Stour contact the National Rivers Authority,
☎ 0732 838858

GOLF

Court Lodge Down
Neville Golf Club
Day tickets available on site.
☎ 0892 27820

WALKING AND RAMBLING

A Circular Promenade
1½ hour or 45-minute walk. Leaflet from the Tourist Information Centre.

Cumberland Walk
Town footpath to open country.

Special Interests

ART GALLERIES

Tunbridge Wells Museum and Art Gallery
Civic Centre, Mount Pleasant
Range of temporary exhibitions.
☎ 0892 26121

FOOD AND DRINK

Penshurst Vineyards
Grove Road, Penshurst
Vineyards and winery, own-label wine.
Wallabies, sheep and black swans in the
grounds. Guided tours by arrangement.
☎ 0892 870255

GARDENS

Owl House Gardens
On the A21
Year-round floral displays, woodlands,
sunken water gardens.
☎ 0892 890230

Penshurst Place
North-west at Penshurst
Walled gardens and parkland with nature
trail.
☎ 0892 870307

HERITAGE

Bayham Abbey
On the B2169
Remains of a 13th century abbey beside
the River Teise.
☎ 0892 890381

Eynsford Castle
Eynsford
11th century Norman castle ruins.
☎ 0892 548166

HISTORIC BUILDINGS

Hornes Palace Chapel
Appledore
Chapel erected in 1366 and consecrated
in 1386.
☎ 0892 548166

King Charles the Martyr
London Road
Fine plasterwork by Henry Doogood.

HISTORIC HOUSES

Penshurst Place
Originally a mediaeval manor house,
developed over the centuries to a
magnificent country house. Toy
museum, gardens, venture playground.
☎ 0892 870307

MUSEUMS

A Day at the Wells
The Corn Exchange, The Lower Pantiles
Walk-through scenes of living history
from the 18th century.
☎ 0892 546545

Penshurst Place
Toy Museum
☎ 0892 870307

David Salomon's House
Broomhill Road, Southborough
19th century house contains
memorabilia of the first Jewish Lord
Mayor of London.
☎ 0892 515152

**Tunbridge Wells Museum and Art
Gallery**
Local history, archaeology and
woodwork, dolls and toys.
☎ 0892 26121 ext 3171

THEATRES

Trinity Theatre and Arts Centre
Church Road
☎ 0892 544699

Water Sports

SWIMMING

Sports and 'Y' Centre
St John's Road
☎ 0892 540744

Rye

Rye was once a busy port, but the sea gradually receded and left it high and dry. Now
some two miles inland, Rye is a very pretty town with cobbled streets and many
lovely Elizabethan buildings, some of which hide behind Georgian frontages. There is
a bow-fronted Apothecary's Shop in the High Street and the Mermaid Inn was
frequented by smugglers during the 18th century. The town was heavily defended
against French raids and had a strong wall with four gates – one of which, the Land or
North Gate, survives. In front of Ypres Tower is the Gun Garden in which the town's
main artillery defences were positioned.

Historic houses in the area include Great Dixter, Brickwall House and Lamb
House which was once the home of author Henry James.

i Rye Heritage Centre
Strand Quay
☎ 0797 226696

Market days Wednesday, Thursday
Early closing Tuesday
Population 4299

Outdoor Leisure

FISHING

Coarse Fishing

Pett Pools
☎ 0424 52678

Powdermill Water
☎ 0580 88407
☎ 0483 570419

Special Interests

ART GALLERIES

Rye Art Gallery
107 High Street
Two galleries linked by a courtyard
garden. Visiting exhibitions and a large
permanent collection.
☎ 0797 222433/223218

FARM PARKS

The Children's Farm
On the A2088 at Beckley
Working farm, milking, shearing,
lambing, harvesting, hop-picking,
working blacksmith and craft shops.
☎ 0797 26250

GARDENS

Brickwall
On the A28 at Northiam
Formal gardens, 18th century bowling
alley, chess garden and sunken topiary
garden.
☎ 0797 223329

Great Dixter
On the A28 at Northiam
Gardens designed by Edwin Lutyens
with topiary, flower borders and meadow
gardens.
☎ 0797 253160

HERITAGE

Landgate
Rye's original town walls.

HISTORIC BUILDINGS

Camber Castle
Built by Henry VII in 1539. Not open to
the public.

Mermaid Street
Well-preserved and picturesque street of
historic buildings.

HISTORIC HOUSES

Brickwall House
Jacobean house with 17th century
plaster ceilings. Now a school.
☎ 0797 223329

Lamb House
West Street
Georgian house, home of the writer
Henry James and, later, author E F
Benson. Some of Henry James' furniture
and possessions remain.
☎ 0797 223763

MUSEUMS

Rye Heritage Centre
Strand Quay
The history of Rye brought to life with
a town model; sound and light show.
☎ 0797 226696/223902

Ypres Tower Museum
Cinque Ports Museum housed in 13th
century defence tower, Rye's oldest
structure.

NATURAL HISTORY

Rye Harbour Nature Reserve
Marsh, shingle, rivers and seashore;
hide available.

RAILWAYS

Kent and East Sussex Steam Railway
Northiam Station
Newly refurbished station terminus for
standard gauge steam railway.
☎ 058 06 2943

ZOOS

The Children's Farm
On the A2088 at Beckley
Domestic and wild animals, birds and
butterflies in 600 acres.
☎ 0797 26250

Water Sports

WATER-SKIING

Rye Water-Ski Club
Rye Harbour Ski Area
☎ 0797 32181

Adjoining Hastings, this seaside town was laid out by James Burton in 1828 and a good many of his original buildings can be seen on either side of St Leonards Gardens. It rapidly became a fashionable, if exclusive, resort after Queen Victoria stayed here. Today it is a tranquil, well-preserved town with a number of attractions including horse-drawn carriage trips. Regular town walks are organised by the Burton's St Leonards Society to discover the town's history.

i 4 Robertson Terrace
Hastings
☎ 0243 718888

Outdoor Leisure

GOLF

Beauport Park Golf Club 🏌18
Battle Road
Visitors welcome without reservation.
☎ 0424 852981

Special Interests

ART GALLERIES

Photogallery
2 Shepherd Street
☎ 0424 440140

FESTIVALS AND FAIRS

August
National Town Criers' Championship

GUIDED TOURS

Burton's St Leonards Society
Free conducted walk with a member of the society – June to August, every Thursday at 2.15 pm. Assemble outside the Royal Victoria Hotel.

ORNAMENTAL PARKS

St Leonards Gardens
Quarry Hill

THEATRES

Marina Pavilion
Seafront
Lively venue for music and dancing.
☎ 0424 712281

Water Sports

YACHTING

Hastings & St Leonards Sailing Club
Low Parade Marina
☎ 0424 813202 Mr Hatch

Sandwich was one of the original Cinque Ports – towns given special privileges by Edward the Confessor in exchange for providing ships and men to transport the Royal Family and its entourage across the Channel. In mediaeval times Sandwich was one of the most important harbours on the south coast, but over the centuries the River Stour has silted up and left the town some two miles from the sea.

Today Sandwich is a quiet market town with a coastal character that has hardly changed over hundreds of years. The streets are narrow, with many Tudor and Elizabethan houses and pretty gabled buildings. Attractions for the visitor include a toy museum, a castle on an offshore island and a restored windmill.

i ✳ St Peter's Church
Market Street
☎ 0304 613565

Market day Thursday
Early closing Wednesday
Population 4500

Outdoor Leisure

CAMPING AND CARAVANNING

Sandwich Leisure Park
Woodnesborough Road
28 pitches for tents, 72 pitches for
touring caravans, 10 pitches for motor
caravans.
☎ 0304 612681

FISHING

River Stour
Good fishing in the summer months
between Plucks Gutter and Grove
Ferry. Canterbury and District Angling
Association permit obtainable from
bailiffs.

Stonar Lakes
Large saline gravel pits stocked with
carp and rudd. Obtain tickets in
advance from local tackle shops, the
charge from the bank is double.

Special Interests

HISTORIC BUILDINGS

White Mill Folk Museum
Ash Road
1760 restored windmill with original
machinery, and a folk museum.
☎ 0304 612076

Richborough Castle
Roman fortress on offshore island, built
when the marshes were still
underwater, and connected to London
by Watling Street.
☎ 0304 612013

St Clement's Church
Knightrider Street
Features a 15th century font.

Strand Street
Fine timber-framed buildings include
Weaver's Houses and The King's Arms.

MUSEUMS

The Precinct Toy Museum
38 Harnet Street
120 years of toys, dolls and miniatures.
☎ 0843 62150

Sandwich Guildhall and Museum
Cattle Market
Victorian photographs, a thumb press
and other artefacts.
☎ 0304 617197

SUSSEX / **Seaford** SUSSEX /

Seaford is a town that used to be a port until its waterway disappeared. In 1579 the
course of the River Ouse was diverted leaving Seaford harbour high and dry. The town
was developed as a seaside resort in the early 19th century. Good walks are to be had
in the downlands around the town and there are fine views of the Seven Sisters cliffs
from Seaford Head.

i Station Approach
☎ 0323 897426

Early closing Wednesday
Population 16,652

Indoor Sports

LEISURE CENTRES

Downs Leisure Centre
Sutton Road
Sports hall, health suite, café and bar.
☎ 0323 490011

Outdoor Leisure

HORSE RIDING

Gatewood Stables
The Barn House, Robin Post Lane,
Wilmington
Instruction in riding and jumping.
☎ 032 12 3709

Special Interests

COUNTRY PARKS

Seven Sisters Country Park
Exceat
Downland, forest and river walks,
information centre.
☎ 0323 870280

HISTORIC BUILDINGS

St Leonards Church
Early Norman church with interesting
13th century capitals.

MUSEUMS

Seaford Museum of Local History
Tower 74, Esplanade
Converted Martello tower with local
history and maritime displays,
collections of early office equipment,
domestic appliances and home
entertainment.
☎ 0323 898222

NATURAL HISTORY

The Living World
Seven Sisters Country Park
Two restored Sussex barns with living
displays of insects from around the
world, and marine and freshwater fish.
Observation beehive and photographs.
☎ 0323 870100

Outdoor Leisure

FISHING

Sea Fishing
Good fishing from the beach.

TENNIS

Salts Recreation Ground
The Seafront

Seaford and Blatchington Tennis Club
Contact Mrs Agar.
☎ 0323 892822

WALKING AND RAMBLING

Cliff Walks
From the seafront, follow the coastal
path to Seaford Head for views of
Beachy Head and the Seven Sisters.

Seven Sisters Country Park
Forest and river walks.

Water Sports

SWIMMING

Seaford Head Pool
Arundel Road
☎ 0323 897632

KENT · Sevenoaks · KENT

A dozen or more historic houses, castles, gardens and monuments can be found close
to Sevenoaks. The most spectacular of these is Knole, built by the Archbishop of
Canterbury in 1456.

i Buckhurst Lane
☎ 0732 450305

Market days Wednesday, Saturday
Early closing Wednesday
Population 24,588

Indoor Sports

LEISURE CENTRES

Wildernesse Sports Centre
Seal Hollow Road
☎ 0732 451437

Multi-Activity Holidays

SPECIAL INTEREST CENTRES

Samuel Palmer School of Fine Art
Reedbeds, Shoreham
Painting holidays.
☎ 095 92 2035

Outdoor Leisure

BIRDWATCHING

Bough Beech Nature Reserve
☎ 0732 75624

174

FISHING

Coarse Fishing
For information and permits contact
the National Rivers Authority.
☎ 0732 838858

GOLF

Knole Park
Seal Hollow Road
☎ 0732 452150

HORSE RIDING

**Bradbourne Riding and Training
Centre Ltd**
Bradbourne Vale Road
Hacking, instruction in riding and
jumping and tuition to BHSAI
standard.
☎ 0732 453592

Chelsfield Riding School
Church Road, Chelsfield, Orpington
Specialise in teaching children, general
instruction, handicap riders and livery.
☎ 0689 855603

Eaglesfield Equestrian Centre
West Yoke, Ash
Instructional residential holidays.
☎ 0474 873925

TENNIS

Hollybush Lane Recreation Ground

WALKING AND RAMBLING

**Sevenoaks Group Ramblers'
Association**
25 St Georges Street

Special Interests

FARM PARKS

Great Hollanden Farm
Mill Lane, Hildenborough
Survival centre for endangered species
of farm animals.
☎ 0732 832276

FESTIVALS AND FAIRS

June
Summer Festival includes music,
drama, dance and children's events.
☎ 0732 455133

July
Sevenoaks Cricket Week

September
Riverhead Carnival

GARDENS

Great Comp Garden
Borough Green
7 acres of formal gardens.
☎ 0732 883889

Knole
Southern end of Sevenoaks town
Formal gardens and deer park. National
Trust.
☎ 0732 450608

Riverhill House Gardens
River Hill
Roses, rhododendrons, azaleas, bluebell
wood, trees and shrubs.
☎ 0732 452557

GUIDED TOURS

Trust Tours
26 Amherst Road
Day tours to stately homes, castles and
gardens in Kent and Sussex.
☎ 0732 451731

HISTORIC HOUSES

Ightham Mote
Off the A227 at Ivy Hatch
Moated mediaeval manor house,
remodelled in 16th century with
impressive painted ceiling in chapel
and Jacobean fireplace in drawing room.
☎ 0732 810378

Knole
Southern end of Sevenoaks
Home of the Sackville family since
1603 and one of England's largest
houses. Built in 1456. Magnificent
furnishings, important art collection,
deer park and gardens.
☎ 0732 450608

Knole

MUSEUMS

Sevenoaks Museum
Sevenoaks Library, Buckhurst Lane
Story of Sevenoaks with commercial,
domestic and trade artefacts and
photographs.
☎ 0732 452384/453118

NATURAL HISTORY

Bough Beech Nature Reserve
Winkhurst Green, near Ide Hill
Kent Trust for Nature Conservation.
☎ 0732 75624

Sevenoaks Wildfowl Reserve
135 acres of lakes, ponds, woodlands
and reedbeds with nature trail and hides.
☎ 0732 456407

THEATRES

Stag Theatre
London Road
Theatre and cinema.
☎ 0732 450175

Water Sports

SWIMMING

Sevenoaks Swimming Centre
Buckhurst Lane
☎ 0732 741712 extn 414

Feeding the deer at Knole

A mile and a half of outstanding views over the busy Thames estuary can be enjoyed
from the promenade at Sheerness. There are traditional seaside amusements in the
seafront gardens.

i Bridge Road Car Park
☎ 0795 665324

Market day Tuesday
Population 11,084

Indoor Sports

LEISURE CENTRES

Sheppey Leisure Complex
The Seafront
☎ 0795 668061

Outdoor Leisure

BIRDWATCHING

Elmley Marshes Nature Reserve
Kingshill Farm, off the A249
Redshank, lapwing, pochard and
shoveler nest in these protected
marshes. Hen harriers and many species
of wader can be seen near RSPB hides.

Special Interests

MUSEUMS

Battle of Britain Lace Panel
Sheppey Leisure Complex
Lace panel depicting the bombing of
London during the Battle of Britain,
permanently on view to the public.

Rose Street Heritage Centre
Reconstruction of a dockyard worker's
home in an 18th century town cottage.
☎ 0795 875047

NATURAL HISTORY

Elmley Marshes
Kingshill Farm, off the A249

Water Sports

WINDSURFING

Barton's Point
Marine Parade
Hire and tuition.
☎ 0795 661187

Shoreham is a busy commercial port and industrial centre at the mouth of the River Adur. It offers a sand and shingle beach and a wealth of maritime history exhibited at the Marlipins Museum.

Market day Saturday
Early closing Wednesday
Population 20,827

Aerial Sports

FLYING

Mercury Flying Club
Shoreham Airport
☎ 0273 462277

Southern Aero Club
Shoreham Airport
☎ 0273 462457

Southern Air
Shoreham Airport
☎ 0273 461661

Outdoor Leisure

BIRDWATCHING

British Trust for Ornithology
83 Buckingham Road
☎ 0273 452472

CAMPING AND CARAVANNING

Harwoods Farm
Henfield
☎ 0273 492820

FISHING

Coarse Fishing
For information and permits for fishing on the River Darent contact the National Rivers Authority.
☎ 0732 838858
☎ 0323 762691
☎ 0734 535000

Sea Fishing
Contact the Tourist Information Centre for details.
☎ 0273 23755

Special Interests

ARTS AND CRAFTS

Henfield Woodcraft
Harwoods Farm, Henfield
☎ 0273 492820

MUSEUMS

Henfield Museum
Village Hall, High Street, Henfield
Local village life and farming museum.
☎ 0273 492546

Marlipins Museum
Local history, paintings and ship models in 12th century building, reputedly the oldest secular building in England.
☎ 0273 462994

Sissinghurst is famous for the gardens created by Vita Sackville-West and her husband Sir Harold Nicolson, considered by many to be the best in Kent. There is also a fascinating farm museum at Staplehurst.

Outdoor Leisure

HORSE RIDING

Appletree Stables
Starvenden Lane, Cranbrook Common, Cranbrook
General instruction, childrens tuition, breaking, schooling, hacking and livery.
☎ 0580 713833

Special Interests

GARDENS

Sissinghurst Castle Garden
Garden created by Vita Sackville-West and her husband Sir Harold Nicolson in the 1930s. Spring garden, white garden, herb garden, rose garden and orchard.
☎ 0580 712850

HISTORIC HOUSES

Sissinghurst Castle
Tudor buildings and tower, the ruins of a 16th century castle. Formerly the home of Vita Sackville-West. Her study in the gatehouse is complete with books, letters, diaries and photographs. In the room above is a manual printing press on which the first edition of T S Eliot's *The Waste Land* was produced by Leonard and Virginia Woolf.
☎ 0580 712850

MUSEUMS

Brattle Farm Museum
Staplehurst
Country museum featuring vintage cars, motorcycles, tractors and wagons.
☎ 0580 891222

At the centre of Kentish cherry-growing country, Sittingbourne is situated on a cree of the River Swale. Close to the old Roman Watling Street, it began to grow i importance at the time of the pilgrimages to Canterbury. Visitors to the town toda can enjoy birds and wildlife at a nearby nature reserve or take a trip on a stea railway.

Market days Friday, Saturday
Early closing Wednesday
Population 36,059

Indoor Sports

LEISURE CENTRES

The Swallows
Central Avenue
Sports hall, squash courts, health suite, sauna, jacuzzi, weights room.
☎ 0795 420420

Outdoor Leisure

BIRDWATCHING

Queendown Warren Nature Reserve
Green woodpeckers, yellowhammers, song thrushes and warblers. Contact the Kent Trust for Nature Conservation.
☎ 0622 53017

FISHING

Coarse Fishing
For information and permits contact
the National Rivers Authority.
☎ 0732 838858
☎ 0323 762691
☎ 0734 535000

Special Interests

ARTS AND CRAFTS

Oad Street Craft Centre
Oad Street, Borden
Work in progress includes woodcraft,
pottery, flower design, upholstery,
knitting and furniture restoration.
☎ 0795 843130

FARM PARKS

Gore Farm
Upchurch
Farm trail, shops and dairy.
☎ 0634 388856

FOOD AND DRINK

Syndale Valley Vineyards
Newnham
Red and white wines produced in a
modern winery. Guided tours.
☎ 0795 89 711/693

MUSEUMS

Bradbury House Victorian Museum
70 High Street, Milton Regis
Extensive collection; Victorian parlour,
drawing room and bedroom.
☎ 0795 423762

Dolphin Yard Sailing Barge Museum
Working barge dock.
☎ 0795 424132

Old Court Hall Museum
High Street, Milton Regis
Timbered mid-15th century building
with local history and arachaeology.
☎ 0795 424341 Borough Council

NATURAL HISTORY

Queendown Warren Nature Reserve
☎ 0622 53017

RAILWAYS

**Sittingbourne and Kemsley Light
Railway**
Steam hauled narrow gauge railway.
☎ 0795 424899
☎ 0634 52672

Water Sports

SWIMMING

The Swallows
Large pool, beach area, flume and
wave-making machine.
☎ 0795 420420

Steyning is a charming little town at the foot of the South Downs, with a long main
street lined with old houses. There is a quaint old clock tower in which George Fox,
founder of the Quaker movement, is said to have held a meeting in 1655.
Bortherwood Hall dates from 15th century and the church displays magnificent
Norman workmanship. The nearby Woods Mill Countryside Centre offers a
fascinating day out for all the family.

Outdoor Leisure

HORSE RIDING

West Wolves Riding Centre
Ashington
General instruction, livery, hacking in
woodland and regular shows.
☎ 0903 892798

Special Interests

GUIDED TOURS

West Sussex History Tours
St Botolphs Cottage, Botolphs
Join Janet Pennington on a tour of
interesting and unusual places in
Sussex.
☎ 0903 879317

179

HISTORIC HOUSES

Chantry Green House
18th century house where Yeats wrote many of his poems.

St Mary's House
Bramber
1470 timber-framed house with panelled rooms, carved fireplaces, pictures, furniture and manuscripts.
☎ 0903 816205

St Mary's House, Bramber

MUSEUMS

Steyning Museum
Church Street
Moving to a new, purpose-built building spring 1991. Features Victorian photographs, and exhibits on local architecture and downland flora and fauna.
☎ 0903 813677

NATURAL HISTORY

Woods Mill Countryside Centre
On the A2037 at Henfield
Headquarters of the Sussex Wildlife Trust. 15 acres of mixed habitat with trail guides and a dipping pond. The 18th century water mill has been restored and holds a natural history exhibition.
☎ 0273 492630

A residential town in the Thames Valley with an interesting 18th century church; the tall yew in the churchyard has been associated with Charles Dickens' well-loved novel *Oliver Twist*. As well as the excitement of horse racing, Kempton Park hosts gala events during the summer and at Christmas. There is good fishing in the Thames.

Outdoor Leisure

FISHING

Coarse Fishing
For information and permits for fishing on the Thames contact the National Rivers Authority.
☎ 0734 535000

GOLF

Lakeham Golf Club ⛳
Lakeham reach, Mixnams Lane
Visitors welcome on weekdays only.
☎ 0932 562877

HORSE RACING

Kempton Park
Off the A308, near the M3 jctn 1
Course founded in 1878, hosts flat and national hunt meetings. Spectacular Gala Evening in June features fireworks, fun fairs and music.
☎ 0932 782292

Special Interests

FESTIVALS AND FAIRS

June
Gala Evening at Kempton Park
☎ 0932 782292

December
Christmas Festival at Kempton Park
☎ 0932 782292

GARDENS

The Walled Garden
Sunbury Park, Thames Street
Walled garden with numerous designs and plant collections.

During the 14th century a flourishing wool trade was established in this delightful town which has many attractive old houses in its long High Street. Full of Wealden character and dominated by the tall 15th century tower of its church it is a good centre from which to explore the surrounding countryside.

i ✳ Town Hall
High Street
☎ 05806 3572

Market day Friday
Early closing Wednesday
Population 5712

Outdoor Leisure

HORSE RIDING

Moat House
Benenden
Specialise in preparing students for examinations, general instruction, livery and holiday courses.
☎ 0580 240581

Nelson Park Riding Centre
St Margaret's Road, Woodchurch
General instruction, children's courses, summer camps, livery and hacking.
☎ 0843 822251

Special Interests

FOOD AND DRINK

Harbourne Vineyard
Wittersham
Small, family-run vineyard.
☎ 0797 270420

Tenterden Vineyards
Spots Farm, Small Hythe
8-acre vineyard and winery producing own label wine. Herb garden, self-guided tours.
☎ 05806 3033

HISTORIC BUILDINGS

All Saints Church
Tudely
18th century brick church with stained glass by Marc Chagall.

Bornes Palace Chapel
Appledore
Chapel erected in 1366 and consecrated 10 years later.

Stocks Mill
The Stocks, Wittersham
Post mill dating from 1781, now fully renovated. Museum display.

Woodchurch Windmill
Woodchurch
Restored working Kentish smock mill.
☎ 0233 860535

HISTORIC HOUSES

Smallhythe Place
Small Hythe
16th century half-timbered house, home of actress Dame Ellen Terry for 29 years.
☎ 05806 2334

MUSEUMS

Smallhythe Place
Dame Ellen Terry Memorial Museum. Theatrical memorabilia and personal possessions.
☎ 05806 2334

Stocks Mill
Small museum of bygones and craft tools.
☎ 079 77 537

Tenterden and District Museum
Station Road
Local history and agriculture, Cinque Ports, Colonel Stephens Light Railway.
☎ 05806 3350/4310

RAILWAYS

Kent and East Sussex Railway
Town Station
Standard gauge railway which runs seven miles to Northiam. Exhibition room, rolling stock and video theatre.
☎ 05806 2943

A splendid gatehouse can be seen at the entrance of the Norman castle which once guarded this ancient market town. Originally settled in the Iron Age, the town still includes some old houses, notably the 15th century Chequer's Inn, 16th century Portreeve's House and the 18th century Rose and Crown Hotel.

i Tonbridge Castle
Castle Street
☎ 0732 770929

Market day Saturday
Early closing Wednesday
Population 34,491

Multi-Activity Holidays

MULTI-ACTIVITY CENTRES

Swattenden Centre
Residential and non-residential sports courses for juniors.
☎ 0580 713657

Tonbridge School
Easter and summer holiday coaching courses in many sports and hobbies.
☎ 0732 365555

Outdoor Leisure

FISHING

Coarse Fishing
Gedges Lake
☎ 0892 832700

HORSE RIDING

Riding Farm
Riding Lane, Hildenborough
Instruction in riding and jumping.
☎ 0732 838717

Special Interests

ANTIQUES

Derek Roberts Antiques
Shipbourne Road
Timepieces dating from as early as 1600.
☎ 0732 358986

COUNTRY PARKS

Haysden Country Park
Newly opened 170-acre park; nature trails, fishing, canoeing.

FARM PARKS

Badsell Park Farm
Crittenden Road, Matfield
Rare farm animals, nature trails, picnic areas. Pick your own, farm shop, teas.
☎ 0892 832549

GARDENS

Tonbridge Castle Grounds
Castle Street
Landscaped grounds by River Medway, with audio walk and visual display boards.
☎ 0732 770929

HERITAGE

Tonbridge Castle
Remains of Norman motte and bailey castle with a 13th century gatehouse under restoration.
☎ 0732 770929

Water Sports

BOAT TRIPS

Caxton Tonbridge Waterways
Castle Walk
90-minute cruises along the Medway.
☎ 0732 456918

YACHTING

Chipstead Sailing Club
Contact P Devitt.
☎ 0732 358897

This small town lies to the east of the Ouse Valley and some fine 18th century buildings can be seen in the High Street. The Maiden's Head, in particular, has a good Georgian facade. Also in the town is a rebuilt church with 17th century brass. The largest collection of rolling stock in the South of England can be seen at the Bluebell Railway.

Population 10,938

Outdoor Leisure

GOLF

Piltdown Golf Club 🏌
Off the A272 at Piltdown
Undulating gorse and heather course. Members of another club and holders of handicap certificates welcome. Correct dress mandatory.
☎ 082 572 2389

HORSE RIDING

Canters End Riding School
Hadlow Down
☎ 0825 85213

Special Interests

COUNTRY PARKS

Wilderness Wood
Hadlow Down
61 acres of woodland, timber barn and woodland trail.
☎ 0825 85509

FARM PARKS

Ashdown Forest Farm
Wych Cross
32 acres with over 40 rare breeds of livestock and poultry, three re-erected 18th century barns, collection of farm machinery.
☎ 0825 712040

Heaven Farm
Furners Green
Nature trail and museum.
☎ 0825 790226

Ketches Friendly Animal Farm
Ketches Farm House, Ketches Lane, Sheffield Park
Farm dates back to 1565. Farm animals, donkeys and ponies. Rides. Blacksmith and local artist at work.
☎ 0825 790968

FOOD AND DRINK

Barkham Manor Vineyard
Piltdown
35-acre vineyard and winery. 18th century thatched barn for wine tastings. Garden and 'Piltdown Man' memorial.
☎ 0825 722103

Flexerne Vineyard
Fletching Common, Newick
3½ acres of vines.
☎ 0825 722548

GARDENS

Sheffield Park Garden
Danehill
18th century garden by Capability Brown with five lakes, rare trees and year-round floral displays.
☎ 0825 790655

MUSEUMS

Bridge Cottage
☎ 082571 2632

Heaven Farm Country Tours and Museum
Heaven Farm, Furners Green
Ancient farm buildings with agricultural equipment and tools, parkland and nature trail.
☎ 0825 790226

Lavender Line Steam Museum
Isfield Station
Standard gauge steam train, rolling stock exhibits, museum and shop.
☎ 0825 75515

RAILWAYS

Bluebell Railway
Sheffield Park Station
5 miles of standard gauge steam railway, largest collection of rolling stock in the South of England, museum and shop.
☎ 0825 722370

Lavender Line Steam Museum
☎ 0825 75515

183

Named after the artificial lake created to embellish the landscape around Windsor Park, Virginia Water is a peaceful haven.

Special Interests

GARDENS

Savill Gardens
3 miles north in Windsor Great Park Outstanding 35-acre garden featuring rhododendrons, camellias, magnolias and hydrangeas.

Valley Gardens
Vast landscaped garden on the fringe of Windsor Park features Roman ruins brought here from Tripoli in 1826, and a triangular Folly Tower, Fort Belvedere, which was turned into a residence for George IV 1827–9. Lovely woodland lake covering some 60 acres is surrounded by oaks, beeches and dark conifers.

Walmer Castle was built in the 16th century and is the official residence of the Lord Warden of the Cinque Ports. The Duke of Wellington died here in 1852.

Special Interests

GARDENS

Walmer Castle Gardens
Kingsdown Road
Terraced castle gardens overlooking the Channel.
☎ 0304 364288

HISTORIC BUILDINGS

Walmer Castle
Built by Henry VIII in tudor-rose shape and the official residence of the Lord Warden of the Cinque Ports since the 18th century. Well preserved, with exhibits relating to former Lord Wardens.
☎ 0304 364288

Walton, probably a Saxon settlement, crops up throughout history. The Elizabethans claimed it was the place Caesar crossed the Thames on his second invasion. Henry VIII granted the people two annual fairs but fenced in their land so that he could hunt deer.

i Town Hall
New Zealand Avenue
☎ 0932 228844

Early closing Wednesday

Indoor Sports

LEISURE CENTRES

Elmbridge Leisure Centre
Sunbury Lane
Full range of sporting facilities.
☎ 0932 243863

SQUASH

Elmbridge Leisure Centre
☎ 0932 243863

Outdoor Leisure

CAMPING AND CARAVANNING

Camping and Caravanning Club Site
Field Common Lane, Horsham
100 pitches, good facilities, play area, fishing, canoeing.
☎ 0932 220932

FISHING

Coarse Fishing
For information and permits for fishing on the Thames contact the National Rivers Authority.
☎ 0732 838858
☎ 0323 762691
☎ 0734 535000

GOLF

Burhill Golf Club ⛳₁₈
Burwood Road
☎ 0932 227345

HORSE RIDING

South Weylands Equestrian Centre
Esher Road, Hersham
General instruction.
☎ 0372 463010

Water Sports

SWIMMING

Walton Swimming Pool
Kings Close, off Kings Road
☎ 0932 222984

Charming little town in the North Downs with considerable character. A mecca for those seeking antiques and a starting point for pleasant walks with good views in the surrounding hilly wooded countryside.

Special Interests

ART GALLERIES

Squerryes Court
½ mile west off the A25
Important collection of old masters, especially Dutch, and 18th century English pictures.
☎ 0959 62345

GARDENS

Chartwell
Golden rose walk, lakes with black swans, Sir Winston Churchill's handbuilt wall.
☎ 0732 866368

HISTORIC HOUSES

Chartwell
The home of Sir Winston Churchill
from 1922 until his death. Much as he
left it, with displayed uniforms, medals
and photographs; his studio contains
many of his paintings. National Trust.
☎ 0732 866368

Quebec House
17th century red brick house, home of
General Wolfe. Pictures relating to
family; exhibition on Battle of Quebec.
☎ 0959 62206

Squerryes Court
¹/₂ mile west off the A25
Beautiful William and Mary manor
house built 1681 with collections of
paintings, tapestries, furniture,
porcelain and items relating to General
Wolfe.
☎ 0959 62345

Statue of Sir Winston Churchill, Wester.

Henry VIII had a palace at Oatlands Park, but very little of it has survived. There are
ancient defensive works on St George's Hill, and a tall column on Monument Hill
commemorates a former Duchess of York. For those interested in the history of
motor racing, Brooklands Museum offers a fascinating insight.

Outdoor Leisure

FISHING

Coarse Fishing
For information and permits for fishing
on the Thames contact the National
Rivers Authority.
☎ 0732 838858
☎ 0323 762691
☎ 0734 535000

Leisure Sport Angling
Thorpe Park, Staines Road, Chertsey
For fishing various lakes in the
Chertsey and Weybridge area.
☎ 0932 564872

GOLF

Foxhills Country Club ⛳
Stonehill Road, Ottershaw
Visitors welcome on weekdays only.
☎ 0932 872050

St George's Hill Golf Club ⛳ ⛳
St George's Hill
☎ 0932 842406

Special Interests

MUSEUMS

Brooklands Museum
The Clubhouse, Brooklands
The story of motor racing and aviation
at Brooklands and Weybridge. Open by
appointment only.
☎ 0932 857381

Weybridge Museum
Public Library, Church Street
National, local and social history,
costume and archaeology. Exhibitions.
☎ 0932 843573

Water Sports

CANOEING

Addlestone Canoe Club
Contact David Waine, 42 Franklands
Drive, Addlestone.

Whitstable

This resort in the Thames estuary is famous for its oysters and the quay has many old houses. Whitstable also has a strong railway tradition, the town once boasted the first-ever passenger line, the world's oldest railway bridge and Britain's first tunnel.

i Horsebridge
☎ 0227 275482

Market day Thursday
Early closing Wednesday
Population 27,063

Indoor Sports

LEISURE CENTRES

Sports Centre
Bellvue Road
☎ 0227 274394

SQUASH

Whitstable Squash Club
West Beach
☎ 0227 273806

TEN PIN BOWLING

Whitstable Bowl
Tower Parade
Ten lanes; snack bar, bar.
☎ 0227 274661

Outdoor Leisure

CAMPING AND CARAVANNING

Timberlost Park
Off the A299 at Seasalter
5 pitches for touring caravans,
2 pitches for motor caravans and
0 pitches for tents.
☎ 0227 272270

FISHING

Sea Fishing
Contact J Dean, 55 Borstal Hill,
for details of Whitstable Angling
Society.

GOLF

Chestfield Golf Club
☎ 0227 794411

Special Interests

FESTIVALS AND FAIRS

July
Blessing of the Waters
Oyster Festival
Whitstable Regatta

August
Carnival

FOOD AND DRINK

Oysters
Local speciality celebrated each year at the Oyster Festival.

MUSEUMS

Whitstable Museum
The Foresters Hall, Oxford Street
The history of the local seafaring community.
☎ 0227 276998

THEATRES

The Playhouse
104 High Street
☎ 0227 272042 box office

Water Sports

WATER SKIING

Seasalter Water Ski
Faversham Road
☎ 0227 264784

YACHTING

Whitstable Yacht Club
☎ 0227 272343

Whitstable Harbour

187

The old town of Winchelsea was destroyed by a storm in 1287. In 1288 it became the first 'new town' in the world with streets built to a grid pattern (predating New York by 600 years). It was one of the original Cinque Ports, second only to Dover in naval importance, and the departure point for many of the Crusades.

Winchelsea's influence declined as the sea receded; its access to the sea has now silted up. It is a tourist's delight with fascinating examples of architecture dating back to the 13th century.

Outdoor Leisure

FISHING

Coarse Fishing
For information and permits contact the National Rivers Authority.
☎ 0732 838858
☎ 0323 762691
☎ 0734 535000

Fishing at Pett Pools
☎ 0424 52678

HORSE RIDING

Higham Farm
Chapel Lane, Guestling Green
Facilities and qualified teachers for riders with their own horses.
☎ 0424 812636

Special Interests

MUSEUMS

Winchelsea Court Hall Museum
Local history exhibits in the old town gaol. Contact Mr Humphrey.
☎ 0797 226365

Old Woking, now a village, was a market town in the 17th century. Modern Woking was built on barren heathland after the arrival of the railway in 1838. There are several interesting buildings in the village including a 17th century manor house and the parish church of St Peter. St Nicholas's Church at Pyrford has simple wall paintings dating from 1200. The first mosque ever built in England stands in Oriental Road. This striking, onion-domed place of worship was built in 1889 and was financed by the Begum Shah Jehan, the wealthy ruler of Bhopal State in India. The town also offers good sporting facilities including golf and tennis.

Indoor Sports

LEISURE CENTRES

Horsell Recreation Centre
Horsell High School
☎ 0483 715333

The Winston Churchill Recreation Centre
Winston Churchill School, Hermitage Road, St Johns
☎ 0483 797015

Woking Leisure Centre
☎ 0483 771789

SQUASH

Woking Squash Rackets Club
Arthur's Bridge Road
☎ 0932 866516

Multi-Activity Holidays

MULTI-ACTIVITY CENTRES

Freetime Leisure
Moor Lane
Multi-activity and sports coaching
holidays for children. Easter and
summer camps.
☎ 0483 740242

Outdoor Leisure

FISHING

Coarse Fishing
For information and permits for fishing
on the Thames contact the National
Rivers Authority.
☎ 0732 838858
☎ 0323 762691
☎ 0734 535000

GOLF

Hoebridge Golf Course ↳
☎ 0483 722611

Windlemere Golf Club ↳
Windlesham Road
Driving range.
☎ 0276 858727

HORSE RIDING

Langshot Equestrian Centre
Gracious Pond Road, Chobham
General instruction, hacking, RDA,
dressage training.
☎ 0276 856949

TENNIS

Chris Lane Tennis Centre
☎ 0483 722113

Special Interests

GARDENS

**The Royal Horticultural Society's
Garden**
Wisley
All aspects of gardening with year-
round displays and specialist gardens.
☎ 0483 224234

HISTORIC BUILDINGS

St Lawrence's Church
High Street, Cobham
52-foot high tower and a cat slide roof
sweeping to 8 feet above ground.
Octagonal oak panelled font.

NATURAL HISTORY

Surrey Wildlife Trust
Powell Corderoy Annex, Longfield
Road, Dorking
For details of activities telephone the
Trust headquarters.
☎ 0306 743404

THEATRES

QEII Theatre and Cinema
Old Woking Road, Maybury
☎ 0483 750561

Water Sports

SWIMMING

Pool in the Park
Kingfield Road
☎ 0483 740685

YACHTING

Oystercat Cruises
5 Poundfield Gardens
Sail-where-you-please holidays in
ocean-going catamaran.
☎ 0483 772442

Worthing

Now the largest town in West Sussex, Worthing was only a tiny fishing village in 1798 when George III's youngest daughter, Princess Amelia, came to convalesce. Her royal patronage led to extensive building over the following 14 years and the creation of a fashionable seaside resort which remains popular to this day. The town centre has fine examples of Regency architecture, and a row of 15th century cottages. However, the area has been inhabited since the Stone Age, and Cissbury Ring, on the edge of the golf course, was an Iron Age camp in 300 BC. Worthing incorporates a pair of former villages, Broadwater and Tarring. Two 19th century authors, W H Hudson and Richard Jeffries, are buried in the cemetery of Broadwater Church where a pair of intricately carved late-Norman arches can be admired. Situated at the foot of the South Downs with a pleasant seafront and a long shingle beach, Worthing is a most attractive coastal resort.

i Chapel Road
☎ 0903 210022

i ✳ Marine Parade
☎ 0903 210022

Population 97,400

Indoor Sports

LEISURE CENTRES

Davison Leisure Centre
Selbourne Road
☎ 0903 204668

Worthing Leisure Centre
Shaftesbury Avenue
Health suite, sports hall, sauna, jacuzzi.
☎ 0903 502237

TEN PIN BOWLING

Worthing Bowl
Marine Parade
☎ 0903 30835

Outdoor Leisure

FISHING

Sea Fishing
Good sea fishing from Worthing Pier.

TENNIS

Beach House Park
Brighton Road

Denton Gardens
Brighton Road

Special Interests

ART GALLERIES

Worthing Museum and Art Gallery
Chapel Road
Pictures by Sussex artists, frequently
changing exhibitions.
☎ 0903 39999/204229

ARTS AND CRAFTS

Smugglers Annex
4 miles west of Worthing at Ferring
Gifts and crafts including fishermens
smocks.
☎ 0903 700191

FESTIVALS AND FAIRS

July
Seafront Fayre

FUN PARKS

Brooklands
Gardens, boating lake, go-karting,
miniature railway, pitch and putt,
playground, cafes.

The Lido
Seafront
☎ 0903 213486

GARDENS

Highdown Gardens
Highdown
5-acre chalkpit with flowering shrubs,
rock plants and rose garden.
☎ 0903 501054

HISTORIC BUILDINGS

High Salvingdon Windmill
Furze Road, High Salvingdon
Built circa 1700, currently under
restoration.

MUSEUMS

Worthing Museum and Art Gallery
Local history and archaeology, toys and
dolls, costume.
☎ 0903 39999/204229

ORNAMENTAL PARKS

Beach House Park
Brighton Road
Gardens, pavilion, tennis courts,
bowling green.

Denton Gardens
Brighton Road
Sunken gardens, putting greens and
tennis courts.

Field Place
The Boulevard
Plenty of sports facilities including
netball, bowling and putting.

Marine Gardens
West Parade
Gardens, sports facilities and café.

Steyne Gardens
Seafront
Sunken garden.

PIERS AND PROMENADES

Seafront Promenade
5 miles of seafront with attractive
floral gardens.

Worthing Pier
Deckchairs, fishing, amusement hall.

THEATRES

Assembly Hall
Stoke Abbotts Road
Multi-purpose venue features a
Wurlitzer organ.
☎ 0903 820500

Connaught Theatre
Union Place
☎ 0903 35333

Pavilion Theatre
Marine Parade
☎ 0903 820500

Water Sports

SWIMMING

Aquarena
Brighton Road
☎ 0903 31797

Useful Information

ROAD ROUTES

M2/A2	London to Dover via Canterbury
M3	London to Winchester
M20/A20	London to Folkestone via Maidstone and Ashford
A21	London to Hastings
A23	London to Brighton via Gatwick and Crawley
A24	London to Worthing
A3	London to Portsmouth
A27/A259	Coastal link roads

BUS COMPANIES

Brighton and Hove Bus and Coach Co
☎ 0273 206666
East Kent Road Car Co
☎ 0843 581333
London Country Bus
☎ 0737 242411
Green Line
☎ 081 668 7261
Southdown Motor Services
☎ 0323 27354

MAJOR RAIL ROUTES

Victoria to Dover via Chatham and Canterbury ☎ 071 928 5100
Victoria to Brighton via East Croydon ☎ 071 928 5100
Waterloo to Portsmouth via Woking and Guildford ☎ 071 928 5100
Charing Cross to Folkestone ☎ 071 928 5100
Brighton to Portsmouth ☎ 071 928 5100
Brighton or Folkestone to Midlands and North via Kensington Olympia ☎ 071 928 5100

Brighton ☎ 0273 206755
Canterbury ☎ 0227 454411
Chichester ☎ 0243 774900
Dover ☎ 0227 454411
Folkestone ☎ 0227 454411
Hastings ☎ 0424 429325
Guildford ☎ 0403 62218
Maidstone ☎ 0732 770111
Margate ☎ 0227 454411
Sevenoaks ☎ 0732 770111
Tunbridge Wells ☎ 0732 770111
Woking ☎ 0483 755905

AIR

Gatwick Airport
internal/external flights

SEA

Sheerness to Vlissingen
Ramsgate to Dunkirk
Dover to Calais, Boulogne, Ostend, Zeebrugge
Folkestone to Boulogne
Newhaven to Dieppe

COUNTY COUNCIL OFFICES

Kent County Council
Springfield, Maidstone
☎ 0622 671411

Surrey County Council
County Hall, Penrhyn Road, Kingston-upon-Thames
☎ 0483 518800

East Sussex County Council
County Hall, St Anne's Crescent, Lewes, East Sussex
☎ 0273 481000

West Sussex County Council
County Hall, West Street, Chichester, West Sussex
☎ 0243 777100

TOURIST BOARDS

South East England Tourist Board
The Old Brew House, Warwick Park, Tunbridge Wells
☎ 0892 540766